SOUL RELEASEMENT

ASSISTING SOULS INTO THE LIGHT

BARBARA M. HARDIE

Crystal Clear Publishing
Tolland, Massachusetts
email: barbara@angelconnections.com
www.angelconnections.com

Cover Artwork: Sue Muldoon Images, LLC;
www.suemuldoonimages.com
Layout and Printing: Paradise Copies, Northampton, MA
Editor: Jo Ann Deck

ISBN: 978-0-9837533-1-5
First Printing September 2013

Printed in the United States of America

Disclaimer

Soul Releasement: Assisting Souls into the Light may contain information that opposes traditional beliefs. This is not meant to offend anyone. It
is provided from the author's personal experiences and spiritual perspective.
The author is not a medical practitioner and in no way is providing medical advice or diagnosis, and therefore, strongly encourages anyone strug-
gling with the symptoms of an attachment or any type of depression to first,
foremost and ALWAYS seek professional help. The information provided is
strictly for information purposes only and the author is not responsible for
any actions taken by the reader.

Dedication

I would like to dedicate this book to the many earth-bound, attached and Resting Area souls I had the pleasure of working with in order to give me the experience I needed to be able to do this work and to share it with others through this writing.

I especially would like to thank Whitney Houston for the information she provided regarding her journey after death through all phases of being earthbound, being an attachment, being in the Resting Area, and finally being escorted to Heaven. It expanded my knowledge as to what it is like once we arrive on the Other Side. She is an absolute delight to work with and occasionally visits to practice her communication skills with humans.

Once again I would like to thank my Heavenly Helpers for their guidance and assistance in training me in the Spiritual Soul Releasement Method of assisting souls into the Light. They are:

Jesus/Sananda

Archangel Michael

Jonathan

The Arcturians

It is a pleasure working with them as well. They truly make spiritual growth super easy.

ACKNOWLEDGMENTS

First, I would like to thank those who purchased my first book *Creating Heaven on Earth: A Guide to Personal Ascension* for their positive feedback. It gave me the courage to move forward and write *Soul Releasement: Assisting Souls into the Light.* I originally planned on putting this information into a small ebook which would provide the procedures involved in assisting souls into the Light. However, as I kept adding more details and giving examples, it blossomed into a hard copy book.

My editor, Jo Ann P. Deck of GatherInsight.com, has once again done a marvelous job with the editing. She has a keen eye for "correctness" and minor details as I write as I speak and that is definitely not always correct. I have attended many author teleclasses and live lectures regarding becoming an author and they all say the same thing – "You absolutely need an editor. Don't skip the editing." JoAnn was truly a valuable asset in putting this book together. Again, JoAnn, I thank you and appreciate you so much!

I would also like to thank Sue Muldoon of Sue Muldoon Images, LLC (www.suemuldoonimages.com), who provided the images for the cover. She also is an expert in her field and I appreciate her taking the time from her busy schedule to help me in finding the appropriate images for *Soul Releasement: Assisting Souls into the Light.*

Last, but not least are the many individuals who enlisted my services in helping them to be free of earthbound and attached entities. Without all of you, I would not have gained the expertise I needed to do this work. Thank you!

Soul Releasement:

Assisting Souls into the Light

TABLE OF CONTENTS

**Part III Assisting Souls from the Resting Area into the
    Light**

Part IV Retrieval and Integration of Your Soul Fragments

Part V Whitney Houston's Journey to the Other Side

AUTHOR'S NOTE

The information and procedures included in *Soul Releasement: Assisting Souls into the Light* is being provided for your personal use to help yourself, family and/or clients. It is not meant to be used as a teaching or training tool for others. Thank you!

INTRODUCTION

Many years ago when I first started on my spiritual path, I was still working in the corporate world. I was fortunate in that my office had a view of the well-manicured lawn, trees and flowering shrubbery – a park-like setting. It was so peaceful that when everyone went to lunch, I stayed behind and usually ate in my office. During one of those peaceful lunch hours, I received a signal in the form of "goose bumps" that Spirit wanted my attention. Archangel Michael and Jesus identified themselves and asked if I would be willing to help them. I naturally said "Yes," without even knowing what they wanted me to do. When the higher vibrating Light energies enter your vibration, you feel so good you would agree to anything.

What they asked me to do was to counsel earthbound souls, get them to agree to go to the Light and then Archangel Michael and Jesus would escort them to the Light. I was so thrilled to be asked to serve these two wonderful Light Beings I could have jumped out of my skin. However, upon their departure from my energy vibration, I bounced back to my "logical" human way of thinking -- "Why would Jesus and Archangel Michael need me to help them? They are so much more powerful than I am."

It wasn't long before Archangel Michael returned to let me know that I was right – their energy was more powerful than mine and that is why they needed my help. At their high energy level, they were not able to connect with the souls who decide to stay earthbound. Being in human form and having developed the ability to communicate with Spirit, we are able to connect with the earthbound souls more easily to provide counseling in order to assist them to the Light. There is no further growth for the soul by staying on Earth, therefore, the importance of returning "home" to the Other Side is an absolute necessity.

Obviously, I am only one of many who are doing Soul Releasement work in conjunction with the Beings of Light on the Other Side.

A Brief Look at the History of Soul Releasement

During some minor research on the history of Soul Releasement work, I found that "spirit possession" dates back to the beginning of human occupancy on Earth. Every major religion and/or cultural tradition (Judaism, Islam, Muslim, Zoroastrianism, Christianity, etc.) refers to spirit possession and the necessity for some form of exorcism ritual. These rituals vary from the use of prayers, incantations, holy water, salt, oils, drums, rattles, roses, commands, speaking in tongue, dancing or whatever was necessary to release the entity.

Many times, illnesses both physical and psychological were (and still are) associated with spirit possession from the perspective of the spiritual healer.

During the Middle Ages, there was a resurrection of the belief in demonology. At that time, the treatment of mental illness was left to the clergy as it was believed that evil spirits were the cause of such illness. Hopefully, someday the medical profession and the spiritual healers will unite in their healing efforts.

The New Testament makes reference that Jesus was anointed by God to not only preach the gospel, but to cast out demons and lay hands on the sick so that they would recover from their illness. Jesus in turn anointed his twelve disciples to preach the word of God and to have the power and authority to cast out demons and to heal the sick. In the days of Jesus, the ability to cast out evil spirits was a sign of true discipleship. Today anyone can perform this act if they so desire.

In medieval times the clergy, in an effort to help possessed individuals, performed depossession or exorcism rituals. If using the cross, prayer and/or holy water didn't accomplish the mission of releasing the attachment, one of the more severe (medieval) methods was to actually beat the host in order to get the attached entities to release themselves. However, according to my guidance, this is not an effective method and created not only physical, but emotional and psychological scars for the host.

The Shaman Healers were the first to recognize the possibility of an earthbound soul's energy attaching to a human (referred to as a host) in order to be able to continue physical life, and as a result, the first to do the releasement work that is common today. An attachment does not necessarily have to be evil or demonic or to intend harm for the host.

The medicine men (salesmen not healers) had their own remedies to get rid of "evil" spirits. These were either potions you drank or gadgets you used to drive the evil spirits away. They travelled from city to city selling their remedies, which usually didn't work. If they were effective it was a matter of your thoughts create your reality and if the buyer "thought" it would work, then it might.

A gentleman by the name of Marcel Vogel created his own method of releasing attached entities by using crystals as a type of surgical tool to release and breakup the attachment. However, upon being released, the energy was able to reunite, not only with itself, but with the host as well. This energy was not escorted to the higher realms by a Light Being, therefore, by remaining earthbound had the freedom to do as it wished.

Most recently (approximately 1950's) hypnosis has been the most popular method of doing this work. Irene Hickman and Bill Baldwin are two individuals (now deceased) who made great strides with the releasement process through the use of hypnosis. When I became a hypnotherapist and learned that method of Spirit Releasement, I decided it was too theatrical for me. During a hypnosis session, the hypnotherapist uses the host (or possibly a medium) as a channel for the attachment to speak through in order to get information as to who they were, when, where and why they attached to the host and other information that may be pertinent at the time of the session. For stage purposes, this was important and very impressive for the audience.

My Own Spiritual Training

I have not had any "formal" (earth classroom) training in this area, but I have had excellent spiritual training. Since Soul Releasement work is something I had included in my Life Plan, my Spiritual Guidance (Jesus/Sananda, Archangel Michael and my Master Guide, Jonathan) have worked with and trained me to use the Spiritual Method of Soul Releasement. They stressed the IMPORTANCE of convincing the attachment(s) to release from the host's energy and get them to agree to be escorted to the Light where they need to be. It was NOT important who they were, when, where, how and why they attached to the host. Sometimes this information is automatically revealed during a counseling session, but it is not necessary.

Getting these entities into the Light is important and necessary whether they are earthbound or attached to a host. The attached entities still have Free Will and cannot be "forced" to go to the Light and this is why counseling is necessary. When they agree, then the Beings of Light will bring them to where they are assigned – the dimensional level depending upon the spiritual growth they achieved during this lifetime or to the Resting Area.

The Resting Area is a temporary location for souls who have a lot of negative energy attached to them as a result of the stressful situations they experienced during their physical life. If they do not agree to go, they have to release from the host and not re-attach to the host or any other human, but they are allowed to stay earthbound if that is their wish.

There are four procedures outlined in *Soul Releasement: Assisting Souls into the Light*:

- Assisting Earthbound Souls into the Light
- Assisting Attachments into the Light
- Assisting Souls from the Resting Area into the Light
- Retrieving and Integrating Your Soul Fragments

These procedures will be explained throughout the various sections of *Soul Releasement: Assisting Souls into the Light*.

"Soul" Releasement

One thing I would like to clarify is my use of the terminology "Soul" Releasement instead of "Spirit" Releasement, which so many before me have used. My interpretation of the difference between Soul and Spirit is that soul energy is that Divine energy within our physical body that continues on and returns to the Other Side after the physical body passes. The Spirit part of us resides on the Other Side in the 7th dimension. Since it is our soul energy which can stay earthbound after physical death, I have been guided to use the word "Soul," the Divine part of us having experiences here on Earth for spiritual growth purposes. Our Higher Self (Spirit) resides in the higher realms of Light to guide us along our spiritual path. This is just a small technicality which I had to adjust to, as I was so used to referring to this work as Spirit Releasement.

While I do this work with the assistance of my Spiritual Guidance, I do charge a fee when I am requested to do releasement work for individuals and/or homes or businesses. Many times individuals are guided to have a reading with me without knowing why. During the reading, a deceased (earthbound) loved one will accompany the client and make themselves known. Then I know why the client was guided to me. I immediately do the counseling work, then the earthbound soul can be escorted to the Light. Or the client may have attachments which are released during the reading and escorted to the Light.

However, there are times when my Spiritual Guidance directs me to a specific location and there is obviously no monetary payment and I definitely don't expect anything. However, the Universe always rewards our actions in their own way (their form of payment) and in their (Divine) time. Much of my payment from Spirit has been given in improved health/healing. This is something that money can't buy and I am very grateful for the blessings I have received.

THE SIDE EFFECT OF SPIRITUAL GROWTH

Another wonderful side effect of humans helping earthbound souls to the Light is spiritual growth. Since spiritual growth is the reason for being in human form, why not assist the souls that are having a hard time making the transition from physical to non-physical? It's a win-win situation for everyone.

In order to use the Spiritual Method of Soul Releasement, it is important to be able to connect with your Spiritual Guidance assigned to assist you during your journey on Earth. Ask if this work is something you are destined to do and if they would be willing to help you. If so, I wish you much success. It is not difficult, but it does take love, compassion, and patience in working with these "lost" souls.

PART I

ASSISTING EARTHBOUND SOULS INTO THE LIGHT

Chapter 1

WHY SOULS STAY EARTHBOUND

MILLIONS OF EARTHBOUND SOULS WHOSE BODIES HAVE passed remain on the planet, some lost, some confused, some angry and defiant. It is not an automatic process that the soul arrives in Heaven upon its departure from the physical body.

Through my Spiritual Guidance, I've learned many reasons why an individual soul decides to stay earthbound once the physical life has ended. Following are some of the common causes:

Fear, especially the fear of going to hell. This is the most common reason. Life on Earth can be very tough and many souls don't want to take a chance, so they stay where they are familiar.

Lack of Awareness of Consciousness after Physical Death. Those who believe that consciousness ceases upon death also think they are still alive when they discover that they have consciousness upon death. It takes some time for the soul to make the adjustment, but in the meantime, the soul stays earthbound.

Manner of Death. Traumatic, sudden, accidental or unexpected deaths create confusion for the soul and the soul thereby decides to stay earthbound.

Desire to Stay Near Loved Ones. Do not ask a loved one who is nearing death to NOT leave you. They have no control over whether they live or die. The soul is in charge of our departure. If they promise you they won't leave you, most likely their soul will stay earthbound.

Fear of Light. If death is caused by fire or an explosion, there is a possibility the soul will choose to stay earthbound.

Familiar with the Earth Plane. Again, the mystery of what lies beyond Earth causes some souls to stay earthbound.

Life Mission not Fulfilled. If a soul feels unfulfilled upon death, it may decide to stay earthbound and try to complete their mission.

Suicide. Most souls who commit suicide stay earthbound because they are in a very confused/disoriented state.

Some Examples from My Releasement Work

Following are a few examples of some of these reasons encountered during my releasement work:

Husband Promised His Wife That He Would Not Leave Her

I was participating in a local psychic fair where photos and descriptions of the type of readings were displayed for the patrons. My specialties are Angel & Soul Purpose readings. Therefore, I was surprised when a beautiful lady, whom I didn't know, sat before me and said that she wanted to know about her husband who had died five years ago. While I usually do not provide information from deceased loved ones, I asked my Spirit Guide if he could provide any information for her regarding her husband. At that point I knew why she was guided to me. Her husband was earthbound, and it was time for him to ascend into the Light. When I asked her to pray with me and to give him permission to go to the Light, she said, "NO." I sensed that it gave her a certain amount of comfort knowing he was still around her, even if it was in spirit form. When I explained to her that being earthbound at such a high vibration was not good for him, that he would be able to help her more from being in the Light than being earthbound, she agreed to assist in releasing his Soul to a much better place.

Since that time she has felt his presence, had an opportunity to connect with his energy directly and mentally talks over situations with him. He is able to provide much more comfort from the Light than from staying earthbound.

Even though our loved ones may no longer be in physical bodies, we still have the ability to communicate with them spiritually. Every human has this God-given ability. We just have to take the time to develop it. When we are born we do not have the ability to speak. We have to develop our language skills over many years. I learned to speak with an autistic child, not by using words, but through telepathy. And that is how we communicate with Spirit – telepathically. Telepathy has roots in two ancient Greek words – "tele" meaning distance and "patheia" meaning feeling or perception.

Fear of Light

A friend of mine was in the process of moving her mother into an assisted living facility. She asked if I would go to her mother's apartment before she moved in to check for earthbound entities. There were two entities (husband and wife) who had died on the property as a result of an explosion in a factory where they had worked. Naturally they feared the Light as it seemed that it caused their deaths.

Suicide

When a human commits suicide there is almost a guarantee their soul will remain earthbound. I have counseled many souls who ended their life and we cannot "force" them to go to the Other Side. They still have Free Will. When they do decide to move upward, they are brought to the Resting Area first in order to restore their soul energy to a higher vibration. I have dedicated Part V of this book to Whitney Houston and her journey to the Other Side after her physical death.

Life Mission Not Fulfilled

A great example of this was shown in the movie *The Sixth Sense*. Actor Bruce Willis plays a child psychologist shot by a patient he did not help so the psychologist stayed earthbound to try to help another patient. I love this movie as I did not realize, until the end, that the main character had died and was still trying to fulfill his life mission.

However, there is no reason – no further growth or benefit by staying on Earth after the physical life is over. You have completed your mission, as much as possible, and it is time to go back to your spiritual home. Staying on Earth is as close to "hell" as you are going to get. The soul is stuck in the vibration it was at during death. If the death was traumatic, the soul relives that experience over and over again. What we fear most is what we attract to ourselves. By being released from Earth and escorted to the Light, the soul is able to be restored to a higher vibration. The higher our vibration, the more calm and peaceful the soul is.

Chapter 2

WHERE TO FIND EARTHBOUND SOULS

Earthbound souls can be anywhere, however the most common places are:

Churches,

Hospitals,

Nursing Homes,

Cemeteries,

Battlefields,

Bars,

Plane Crash Sites,

Earthquake Areas, and

Any locations where disasters happen or an individual dies are common places for earthbound souls to reside.

My grandmother loved going to church and walked every day (not just on Sundays) to her nearby church. If her soul had stayed earthbound upon her passing, she would have gone to the church for comfort.

On the other hand, if someone feels more comfortable in

a bar during physical life, that is where their soul would find comfort upon passing. As a matter of fact, my Spirit Guides indicate that if the earthbound entities in bars had physical bodies, the walls would probably explode.

The Heavenly Helpers need our assistance in getting these lost souls to the Light (our spiritual home) where they belong. Archangel Michael and Jesus/Sananda asked if I would help them retrieve earthbound souls and assist them in returning to their spiritual home in the higher realms. While the energy of my Spiritual Guides was with me, what they were requesting seemed so logical, so right and I was honored to be chosen as a helper in this mission. However, when I was alone with my own energy, I felt foolish to think that Jesus/Sananda and Archangel Michael would need my help as they were so much more powerful than I was. So I dismissed their request for help. Archangel Michael came to me in meditation once again and explained that I was correct – their energy was at a higher vibration than mine; however, the earthbound soul energy was lower than mine and, therefore, I would act as a go-between. Spirit needed to work through human energy on Earth to connect with the earthbound souls, as they were not able to make the connection from their energy level in the higher dimensions. This made sense to me, and I have been assisting them with helping earthbound souls to return to their spiritual home for the past 20 years.

Initially, when I was guided to do Soul Releasement work, I went to cemeteries, churches and other areas where earth-

bound souls congregate. I mentally called out to any earthbound souls to come forward for counseling and passage to the
Light/Heaven. I would answer any questions they had. One of
the most common concerns was whether or not they would
be admitted to Heaven. Many souls believe that if they did
anything wrong, no matter how minor, that they would go to
"hell," not Heaven. They weren't going to take any chances, so
they stayed earthbound because they were familiar with Earth.
Unfortunately, what they didn't know was that by remaining on
earth after physical death was as close to "hell" as they could
ever experience. So what they were trying to avoid is what they
immersed themselves in. Always, always remember to go with
your Angels or Spirit Guides upon physical death, as it is their
responsibility to bring you where you need to be.

As I became more experienced, I was guided to distant
areas:

New England,

New York,

Florida,

Japan,

Caribbean,

Spain,

Israel,

Greece,

Bali,

Sedona & All of Arizona, and

Manhattan on 9/11, where I assisted souls from the Twin Towers by creating a portal and counseling them.

What To Do If Loved Ones Want You To Leave Earthbound Souls Earthbound?

An individual was aware of "ghost" activity in her home and called me for help in getting rid of the ghost. When my Spiritual Guides indicated that the entity was her deceased boyfriend, she asked me to stop the process and leave immediately. She wanted him to be with her. She now wanted to get rid of me, not the entity. She was willing to pay me for my services, but didn't want me to proceed any further. Naturally, I left the premises, but handed the situation over to my Spiritual Guides. If it was in the highest interest of the earthbound soul to be escorted to the Light, the Spiritual Guides would help with this transition. It could be that was why he was making himself known, to get assistance to bring him where he needed to be. This young man died as a result of an accident and, therefore, it would have been very natural for his soul to stay earthbound. But there comes a time when the soul needs to be released. It is also natural for loved ones to want their deceased loved ones to be with them here on Earth. However, staying on Earth after the physical body no longer exists is not good for the soul, since no spiritual development can be made, and it is cruel for us to keep them here.

If you encounter a situation such as this, don't argue with the loved ones, just pass the responsibility to the Light Beings you are working with from the Other Side to assist the earth-bound in any way they can.

I encountered a similar situation via a phone call. Basically, someone just wanted me to confirm that they had ghost activity in their home by relaying some of the happenings. Unfortunately, they did not want me to assist the entity to the Light as the activity was a form of their entertainment. People who did not believe in ghosts were invited to come over and experience it for themselves. The happenings caused them to become believers. The caller mentioned that while having dinner at the kitchen table one evening, with lots of people in attendance, a knife from the counter flew across the room by itself. Even though my services were not requested, I reached up to my Spiritual Guidance and asked that they please go to this location and release the entity or entities causing the destructive activity. It was possible that the entity was looking to get their attention in order to get to the Light and became violent as a result of being used as their entertainment.

Again, if you are not able to do anything, pass it on to your Spiritual Helpers and let them do whatever is appropriate.

Soul Releasement at a Distance and on Location

Many times my Spiritual Helpers guide me to locations in order to participate in Soul Releasement work. Sometimes it is necessary to go to the physical location and other times it is appropriate to connect with and guide the earthbound souls via meditation. Here are a few examples:

EARTHQUAKE IN JAPAN

I was just beginning to work with Spirit regarding releasement work at a distance when I heard the news of the earthquake which took place in Japan in 1998. I was extremely naïve at that time, as when my Spiritual Guides asked me to help assist earthbound souls from that disaster to the Light, my response was that I did not speak Japanese. It seemed logical, but actually, it did not matter. During meditation my guides assisted me in connecting with the earthbound souls in Japan. I counseled them in English, and I believe the translation was done by Spirit. Anyway, whatever the process was it worked as many souls transitioned to the Light.

9/11 -- NEW YORK CITY -- TWIN TOWERS

This was a devastating event. My husband and I were glued to the TV when the news broke. He had a business meeting in New Hampshire and asked if I wanted to go with him for the ride. I agreed, but we listened intently to the radio broadcast regarding the planes flying into the Twin Towers. Suddenly, my Spirit Guides were giving me the signal (goose bumps) they wanted to speak to me. At that time, my rule was that they not connect with me unless I was meditating. However, there was an emergency and they needed my help. They asked that I create a portal (a mental creation of an opening to the higher dimensions through a shaft of Light as a passageway for earthbound souls to transition from Earth to the higher dimensions) at the site of the Twin Towers in New York City so that the souls that had passed in that event could be guided to the Light.

So with my eyes closed I started creating the portal and calling forth any and all souls to be guided to the Light through this portal, this passageway of Light.

I am sure Spirit was working with many Light workers in getting souls to the Light. The funny part was my husband had no idea as to what I was doing, but as he looked over at me he noticed that I was crying for no apparent reason. However, when connecting with the earthbound entities, I was feeling what they were feeling and it wasn't good. I put my hand up (as a traffic cop would do to stop traffic) so my husband wouldn't interrupt me. I was surprised that we did not get into an accident as he was more interested in what was happening with me crying than in driving the car. Thank God we had Angels in the car with us. When the process was completed, I opened my eyes, dried them and then explained what I was doing. I think he thought I was "crazy."

Non-Financial Rewards in Barcelona and Jerusalem

BARCELONA, SPAIN

In 2009 I was on a Mediterranean Cruise. The Rheumatoid Arthritis symptoms I was experiencing at that time prevented me from getting off the ship and touring the beautiful countries of Spain, Italy and France. However, my friend and I scheduled an extra few days in Barcelona at the end of our cruise before returning to the airport and home. We visited a few of the churches and cathedrals in the area near our hotel.

I was naturally guided to meditate in these beautiful buildings and to call forward any earthbound entities who wanted passage to the Light.

The first church we visited was open; however, service was not in session. It was absolutely beautiful. After touring and viewing all the pictures and statues, I sat down and began to meditate to call forth any earthbound entities – not only within that church, but throughout all of Barcelona and Spain. Churches are a very common place for earthbound souls to "hang out," as they believe it to be a place of comfort and may feel closer to God in a church. It was early afternoon, and not necessary for the lights to be on inside the church. I was guided to open a portal above the altar as a passageway for the souls to go to the Light. During this meditation I had my eyes closed, but others in the church witnessed a brightening effect as if someone turned on the lights. They also witnessed a stream of Light (portal) above the altar which appeared as if sunlight was shining through a window, but there was no window. When I opened my eyes and spoke to some of the ladies around me, they asked if I had observed the brightening effect and the stream of light above the altar. I had not witnessed what they did, but it confirmed to me that what Spirit guided me to do actually took place. The brightening effect was the exit of thousands of souls who had occupied space within the church. These ladies had no idea that I was doing a Soul Releasement exercise. I'm not sure they would have understood what I meant if I had told them. It was refreshing for me to hear their comments about what they witnessed. At the end of our visit, a total of 8,000 earthbound entities were escorted to the Light from these locations in Barcelona.

My reward from Spirit for not being able to tour Europe on the Mediterranean Cruise and for performing the Soul Releasement exercise in Barcelona was a significant improvement in my Rheumatoid Arthritis symptoms -- increased mobility.

JERUSALEM, ISRAEL

Less than a year later (2010) when I was guided to go on a spiritual pilgrimage to Israel (it was a bus tour and I would not have been able to stay at the hotel if I was having a bad day), I asked Spirit for a special favor – to be able to keep up with the tour every day. I knew my Angels/Spirit Guides had a specific reason for guiding me to this area; however, I was not quite sure what the purpose was before signing up. This is called acting on faith and trust. I thought it could be past life history/ karma I needed to balance out. The Holocaust Museum in Jerusalem was one of our points of interest on this trip. A few days before arriving at the Holocaust Museum, my guides asked if I would assist them with Soul Releasement at that site. Aha, it now made perfect sense. When we arrived at the Museum, I stepped away from the group, found a quiet place to meditate, and called forward as many earthbound entities as possible for passage to the Light. Jesus and Archangel Michael as well as many other Beings of Light were there to assist. I did my routine counseling work and then had to leave as it was time to get on the bus.

We were staying at a monastery in Jerusalem which had
been converted into a hotel. That night after returning to the
hotel, I went to the chapel to pray for the souls that had been
released and hoped they arrived quickly and safely. Mother
Mary came forward and thanked me for the work I had done
and reported that 200,000 plus souls had been released from
Earth during the Releasement Process. I was elated with that
news since in previous releasement ceremonies, only hundreds
and occasionally a few thousand souls had been released.
Mother Mary indicated there were still many who had decided
to stay earthbound. Of course, my time for counseling was
limited as this was a bus trip and when the tour of the museum
was over, the bus had to leave. I had asked our group leader
to make sure the bus did not leave without me. In all of Israel,
the worst place I can imagine being left behind would be at
the Holocaust Museum. Even though I might have been able
to complete the Releasement Process, I preferred to sleep in
the beautiful monastery with the rest of our group. I am sure
Spirit will work with others who have the ability to release
earthbound entities to the Light to continue releasing the many
hundreds of thousands of earthbound entities still in that location. I am open, ready and more than willing to work with my
Spiritual Guides in releasing these souls on a remote basis as
we did with the Japan earthquake and the New York City Twin
Towers victims.

Their gift to me was a miraculous healing. I believe it was
their reward for the work they guided me through, not only

in Spain, but also at the Holocaust Museum. Experiencing improved health is the best payment I could have received. No amount of monetary payment would have been able to "buy" me better health. While I do not expect payment when I am guided by Spirit to do Soul Releasement work, I am more grateful than anyone will ever know for all the blessings that I have received just for doing the "work" I love to do. Spiritual growth is another side benefit for working with our Heavenly Helpers.

Chapter 3

A PROCEDURE FROM MY SPIRITUAL GUIDANCE

Assisting earthbound souls to the Light is part of my Soul Plan/Contract for this lifetime. However, because it is such a major issue, Spirit has guided me to write this "How To" book so that others will be able to help themselves with releasing earthbound entities or help others who may be experiencing "ghost" activity in their areas.

Procedure to Connect with & Counsel Earthbound Souls

Following is the procedure given to me by my Spiritual Guidance when they first began to work through me to release earthbound souls:

1. Always PROTECT yourself. I use the Golden/White Light. Mentally bring down a combination of Golden/ White Light from the 9th dimension and wrap it around your inner and outer bodies for the purpose of

protecting yourself from any negative or earthbound energy attaching to you while doing releasement work. Feel free to continue to use your own protective exercise if that is more comfortable for you.

2. Call upon your Heavenly Helpers – Angels, Spirit Guides, Ascended Masters and Higher (God) Self. You will need someone from the Light to be an escort for the earthbound souls, as they cannot leave the Earth plane without an escort from the Light to guide them. All souls need an escort, even those who rise up automatically upon death.

3. As an additional precaution, ask your Heavenly Helpers to ensure that you are protected from the earthbound entities who may want to attach to your energy.

4. Ask your Heavenly Helpers if there are earthbound entities in the location that you intend to clear, and, if so, how many?

5. If you receive a "yes" response, mentally/telepathically call out for any earthbound soul to come forward for passage to the Light. If they have questions, you will be happy to answer them.

6. Don't be surprised if you don't get a response even though you KNOW that they are there. If there is more than one entity, ask to speak to the strongest (most powerful) one. Usually one will be the spokesman for them all. If there is only one just keep talking until you

get them to respond. This is the start of your counseling session.

7. Usually I am guided by my Heavenly Helpers as to what I say, but some of the usual comments made during a counseling session are:

- Assure them that your only purpose is to help them get to the Other Side where they need to be. Being on Earth without a physical body is as close to hell as they are going to get.

- Tell them there is a better, much better, place for them to be now. They will be able to view their loved ones on Earth from this better place once they are situated.

- No matter what they did while in physical form, God automatically forgives them. God views our wrong-doings as experiences which can be corrected at another time. They need to forgive themselves and anyone who has hurt them. No matter what anyone has done, it is no longer important and they will know this as fact when they return to the higher realms.

- Tell them that some of the most horrific criminals on Earth have made it to Heaven so they will have no problem. The "key" to Heaven is FORGIVENESS of self and others.

- Tell them that the only contraband not allowed in Heaven is negative energy. Encourage them to release and let go of any negative energy they accumulated at the soul level on Earth, and this will bring their energy to a higher vibration and make their transition from Earth to Spirit much easier.

- If they continue to hold onto the negativity, they will be brought to the Resting Area. This is not a bad or evil place. It is a place for the soul to be restored and this can be done through the vibrations of Love, Forgiveness & Compassion.

- There is a possibility that your counseling efforts will be ignored. In that case, if there is only one entity, tell it that an escort will take it to the Other Side and show it around with a guarantee that if the entity is not happy, the escort will bring it back to Earth. If there are a group of earthbound souls, ask one or two to volunteer to go with the escort to view the Other Side and then re-turn with the escort to share with the others what they witnessed. Almost 100% of the time when the entity returns and is excited about where they went and want to go back, the others will follow. (In all the years I have been doing this work, only one time did an entity return to Earth, but promised to go back once they resolved an issue they thought could only be resolved on Earth.)

- Remind them that Earth is a physical planet, and we need a physical body while here. Once the physical body dies, remaining on Earth will be like the hell we all want to avoid. The pull of the Earth's gravity keeps the soul stuck in the vibration it was at the time of death. By going to the Light, souls are relieved of the burdens of Earthly life.

8. Your Heavenly Helpers will let you know when the entity/entities agree to go. At that point you can bid them good-bye or say any parting words that you feel are necessary.

Keep in mind the above procedure is only a guide. Once you connect with your own Spiritual Helpers, be guided by what they suggest is the best process in each situation. On a few occasions, especially in suicide situations, my guidance has closed me down from working with these souls. It may depend upon their level of anger at the time of death and they need time to calm down. I'm not sure, but I have learned to listen as I know the Angelic Helpers KNOW more than I do, and they will give me a heads up if and when it is time to call out to these souls in the future for assistance to the higher realms.

Always remember to protect your own energy when working with earthbound souls so that you do not end up with them as an attachment, which we will cover in the next section.

PART II

ASSISTING SOUL
ATTACHMENTS
INTO
THE
LIGHT

Chapter 4

WHAT IS AN ATTACHMENT?

In 1994 I had attended a workshop hosted by William J. Baldwin, author of *Spirit Releasement Therapy: A Technique Manual.* He indicated that his research revealed that approximately 70% to 80% of humanity either has or will experience soul attachment some time in their life.

According to my Spiritual Guidance, the percentage is closer to 100%. Attachments don't always stay with a person from the time they attach until the death of the host. They are free to come and go and do so frequently depending upon their energy vibration compatibility to the host. Like attracts like energy.

The individuals who attract attachments are people who have lowered their vibration through addictions, such as alcohol or drugs (both street and prescription) or through physical, mental, emotional or spiritual abuse. And last, but not least, are those who are exposed to stress on a regular basis. That accounts for just about every human on Earth.

You do not have to know all the details of when, where, how and why the attachment joined the host. The important thing is to release the attachment and arrange for its passage to the Other Side with the help of your Spiritual Team of helpers – Higher Self, Spirit Guides, Angels, Ascended Masters and/or Jesus/Sananda and Archangel Michael or anyone in the higher realms assigned to work with you.

Definition of an Attachment

When an earthbound soul attaches to an individual's physical body or auric field, it is referred to as an Entity, Soul or Spirit attachment or a Possession. It does not matter what we call this energy, however, technically it is "Soul" energy – the part of Divine energy carried in the human body to experience life on Earth.

An attachment could be a fragment (part) of another person's soul energy or even the entire soul of an individual who passed from a physical body to their energy body and for some reason decided not to return to their rightful place in the higher dimensions, but to continue life by attaching to another human being.

The negative thought forms directed at us from other living humans are referred to as attachments. Depending upon the situation and frame of mind the individual was in when their thoughts were directed at us (usually very negative as a result of anger, rage or stressful vibration), we could "own" this negativity. This is one situation where forgiveness is ultra important in releasing the energy to be returned to its rightful owner, surrounded with the Light and Love of God. I have read articles which state to surround yourself with a mirror-like substance so that these negative thoughts are returned to their owners. I find this process does not transform the negativity, it only shifts it around. God's energy cannot be destroyed. It can only be transformed from positive to negative or from negative to positive. Spiritual growth is involved when we transform the negative to positive. If we have an opportunity to do this and don't – it is definitely a missed opportunity for spiritual growth.

Anything from the outside that is not your own energy that attaches to your energy and has any influence on you is considered an attachment.

Sometimes our own negative thoughts get caught in our energy field. However, this negative energy can be transformed from negative to positive through the use of the White Light, the Violet Flame, or the vibrations of Love, Forgiveness and Compassion. Keep in mind that your own negative thoughts have a negative influence upon your life. If you catch yourself wallowing in negativity, you have the power to turn it to a positive vibration by thinking positive.

Are Attachments Part of Our Soul Contract?

NO! Attachments are NEVER a part of our Soul Contract, so do not feel as though they are there for a reason and you might be learning a lesson as a result of their attachment. The only lesson to be learned from having an attachment is to be sure to check from time to time to make sure that you DO NOT have any energy that is not your own attached to you.

You can do this in meditation by asking your Spirit Guides if you are free of attachments or entities. If not, then you need to release them with the help of the Light Beings. There is absolutely no benefit or spiritual growth to hosting an attachment. It is not only in the highest best interest of the host, but it is best for the earthbound entity to go to the Light.

While it is possible for an earthbound entity to plan their attachment to a physical body, in these rare cases it is usually associated with revenge (the opposite of the Golden Rule – "Do unto others as they have done unto you" or "An eye for an eye"), a get even situation. However, an attachment is NEVER part of a Soul Contract and that is why it is so important to release them.

What's the Difference Between an Attachment and a Possession?

An attachment (earthbound entity) may just hide or nest in the host's energy field, causing no "real" problems for the host except fatigue caused by the lower vibration of the entity connecting with the host. An attachment may take over some, but not complete, control of the host's thoughts, actions, feeling or words. In any case, since our purpose is to grow to the highest spiritual level/vibration possible, we need to release and let go of any energy that is not our own. Whereas a possession is an earthbound entity who, when attached to the host, takes over full control of the host's thoughts, actions, feelings and/or words. While a possession is not as common as an attachment, it does happen. If an individual is burdened with an abnormal amount of negative energy due to circumstances in their life and they feel tired and unhappy, the greater the chances of attracting an entity with a desire to take possession of a physical body.

Attachments don't have to be anyone you know or have karmic issues with. It is a matter of like attracts like energy. Attachments may feel comfortable going along for a ride at your expense. If you are weak, a stronger entity may like the idea of being in control through connecting with you.

Important: under NO circumstances is it acceptable to host an attachment. Also, if you are conscious that you have an attachment, DO NOT become fearful. I know this is easier said than done. Fear is a source of fuel for the attachments. You are feeding them power – your power.

Earthbound Souls Can Also Take Over Possession of Property

Earthbound entities can also take over a location familiar to them and not wanting anyone else to occupy it. This was seen in the movie *Amityville Horror*. Also, an example in my local area was a restaurant where the original owner of the property (farmland) died as a result of an accident on the farm. His soul stayed earthbound on the property upon physical death. Eventually the land was sold and as progress happens, a restaurant was built on the property. This entity created such chaos within the restaurant that it caused the patrons to abruptly leave. The owner of the restaurant decided to close it down. The new "potential" owners decided to enlist the services of a meditation group I belong to in order to clear the property of this entity or entities.

During our meditation at the site, I was able to connect with an entity by the name of Joe who was causing the problem. He tried to be "tough" by telling me that if I and the others didn't leave, he would kill us. Archangel Michael, Jesus and many other Beings of Light were with us that evening and I don't scare easily, so I stood tough as well. I told the entity that we had Jesus and Archangel Michael there to protect us and him. These two angelic beings would be willing to take him to the Light. Earth is a physical planet and without a physical body, he was keeping himself stuck in a hellish place experiencing anger and frustration regarding others occupying "his" property. Legally these intruders now owned the property – the entity no longer had any rights to it. By returning to the Light he would be able to plan a new life, and in that planning stage he could choose any type of life he wanted.

He decided to go with the Beings of Light. I was amazed that only one entity had the power to cause as much chaos as he did single handedly. He was not a bad or evil soul he was just trying to protect what was once his property.

Chapter 5

MY FIRST SOUL RELEASEMENT SESSION

One evening during meditation, shortly after I was prompted to learn and perform Soul Releasement work from my Spiritual Guidance, I decided to check myself for attachments by asking my guides if I was carrying any energy which was not my own. Much to my surprise, I had eight attachments. This gave me the opportunity to practice working on myself first before taking on any clients. I live near a cemetery so I guess it should not have been a surprise that I had attachments.

I now check with my guides on a regular basis to make sure my energy is clear of attached entities, especially when things start going wrong. I assume it can't be me, it must be an attachment. Usually when I am irritable for no reason or I start thinking negatively or I experience curse words popping up in my thoughts, I KNOW I have an attachment(s). It's easy to clear them out because I know what to do, but I feel sorry for those who are having attachment experiences and don't know or think to check with their Heavenly Helpers to see if they are clear of attachments.

The comedian Flip Wilson used to have a saying during his routine – "The Devil Made Me Do It!" Maybe not the devil, but it could have been an attachment.

Chapter 6

SOME REASONS WHY EARTHBOUND SOULS ATTACH TO A HUMAN HOST

When an earthbound soul attaches to a human host, there could be several reasons why. A few of these examples are:

1. The host just happens to be in the area where the earthbound is currently residing, such as a nursing home, hospital, cemetery or a possibility of a million places. Earthbound entities can be anywhere, but the aforementioned are the most common.

2. The earthbound has an addiction of some kind such as, drugs, alcohol, cigarettes, food, sex, etc., and seeks out a human host so that they can continue with their habit through the host. Many times the earthbound entity does not know the host, has never had a connection with the host, and is only attracted for the purpose of continuing life in physical form. Like attracts like energy.

3. The earthbound entity has no intention and most likely doesn't even know that it is possible to attach to a human host to continue life, but accidentally comes too close to a human's energy field, gets "stuck/caught" and decides to stay.

4. Occasionally the earthbound might attach to the host due to unfinished business from physical life; therefore, they would have had a connection with the host from the current lifetime or possibly from a past life.

5. Attachments could be the result of unresolved karmic issues.

   Example: A therapist was working with a young boy and her Spirit Guides gave her the message that the boy had an attachment. She did not know how to deal with that issue so she contacted me. In checking with my Spirit Guides, the boy only had one attachment who happened to be someone he had killed in a past life. The attachment was a male and died at the age of 21 and chose to stay on Earth. When he recognized the soul of the young boy as the same soul who had caused his death in a previous lifetime, he attached to the young boy's energy field with the intent of causing the boy's death at age 21. When I realized the severity of the situation, I did the releasement work immediately.

Even though as humans we have a specific identity (physical body), souls are able to recognize souls so it does not matter what form we take on or where we locate. If the earthbound entity had gone to the Light upon his death, he would have seen things from a different perspective, and the revengeful death through attachment would not have been an option.

When I reported this situation to the therapist, I told her it was up to her what she reported to the boy's mother. I didn't expect the therapist to pay for the releasement session, and because I did not have an agreement with his mother to do the session, I told the therapist there would be no charge for the session. However, if the mother wanted to send me a donation, I would be very appreciative. She sent me $25.00.

I was grateful, however, because it indicated to me the necessity of writing this book to help individuals understand the importance of Soul Releasement work. I also wanted to explain how to do this work so individuals could help themselves and their loved ones.

Because we do not have physical surgical tools and cannot show that anything has been removed, I find people are reluctant to pay for this service. The effects are recognized in how you feel after a releasement session. You should feel more uplifted (lighter), more positive in your thinking and more energetic (higher vibration).

Chapter 7

WHEN EARTHBOUND SOULS ATTACH TO OUR ENERGY

Unfortunately, most humans are not able to "see" earthbound souls and, therefore, are at a disadvantage as to when they attach to our energy field. Following are some possible reasons:

OUR ENERGY IS AT A LOW POINT
This is why it is important to take conscious steps to keep our energy at the highest level possible.

DURING TRAUMA, SEVERE STRESS OR AN ACCIDENT
Again, our energy is at an extremely low point during traumatic/stressful situations, which makes us a perfect candidate to pick up an attachment.

An example: One of my friends came to me for a hypnosis session and wanted to work on one specific issue – weight loss. During her session we got off the subject of weight loss and went into the subconscious mind to find out why she drove so slowly. She thought it was because she came from a town where the terrain was flat and easy driving, different from where she now lived in a hill town with steep, winding, curvy roads. During her session, it was revealed that while she was driving in her former town, there was an accident just ahead of her. Naturally all the traffic stopped and she happened to be the first car in line. They had to wait for the police/ambulance to arrive because there was a fatality. Unfortunately, the man driving the car ahead of her died and when his soul released from his body, it went straight to her and attached to her energy. She had been carrying him around for a few years. During our session I released his soul from her energy, and he was escorted to the Light. This was the good news. The bad news was that this lady received two speeding tickets within the next week following the releasement session. When she told me this fact, I told her I couldn't bring the attachment back to slow her down. She would have to learn to SLOW DOWN on her own. This was proof that, after the accident happened, she was not in control while driving -- the attachment was driving. I'm not sure if speeding was the cause of his accident and ultimate death, but if it was it makes sense that he would want to drive slower to ensure that he did not have to go through that experience again.

During Organ Transplant Surgery

This almost always occurs with organ transplant recipients, especially heart transplants. When I perform the Soul Releasement procedure, I do not go into the details of when, why, where with the attachment so I am not sure if any of the entities I have worked with were from an organ transplant donor. However, the *Journal of New Approaches to Medicine and Health* has printed an article on this subject – "Memory Transference in Organ Transplant Recipients" (Vol. 19, Issue 1, April 24, 2011) which lists many cases of attachments from organ transplants. It can be found at www.namahjournal.com in the Archives section.

Example: I watched a TV special many years ago where they interviewed a woman who had a heart transplant. She ate healthy, exercised and did everything right because she had a "bad" heart. It came to a point where she needed a transplant or her days were numbered. When a young man died in a motorcycle accident, his heart became available to her. She had been in the habit of healthy eating, however, after the transplant she started going to McDonald's and eating "his" favorite foods. At that time, they did not reveal the name of the organ donor to the recipient. However, because some of his soul energy was attached to his heart, she started receiving bits and pieces of information about him, and he eventually led her to his parents' home. They made a movie based on this true story called *A Stranger's Heart* which starred Jane Seymour as the recipient of the heart. Not sure if his energy was ever released from the recipient, but it was an example of an attachment due to transplant surgery.

WHEN WE DON'T PROTECT OUR ENERGY

It is absolutely necessary to daily protect our energy not only from attachments, but from the negativity of other people we have contact with on a daily basis. If you do not already have a protection exercise you use, I have listed the protection exercise I use under Item No. 1 of the "Procedure to Connect with and Release Attachments" in this section.

WHEN WE VISIT LOCATIONS WHERE EARTHBOUND ENTITIES RESIDE

Earthbound souls can reside anywhere, however, the more common areas (also mentioned in Part I) are: churches, hospitals, cemeteries, nursing homes, battlefields, bars, plane crash sites, earthquake areas or any disaster areas as well as the homes they lived in before death. If we take the time to protect ourselves DAILY, we won't have to worry about taking extra energy home with us.

WE MAY INVITE THEM WITHOUT REALIZING IT

This happens when we ask our loved ones not to leave us. Our intention for putting in this request is the "hope" that they will not die. The individual human does not choose death (other than in the case of a suicide). It is the soul that exits according to the timing and circumstances set up in our Life Plan Blueprint. So if an individual promises not to leave and the soul decides it's time to exit, many times the soul will stay earthbound in order to please and to continue to be near their loved ones.

Example: I had attended a hypnosis conference in New Jersey and a gentleman was presenting a workshop on Spirit

Releasement. He told of a session with a lady in a nursing home in his area. Her children arranged for her to be placed in the nursing home after her husband (their father) died. They said she was acting "funny." She was talking to her husband as if he was in the room – asking him what he wanted for dinner, then cooking and eating it herself.

Well, her husband actually was with her as an attachment and he was able to continue to enjoy her cooking and the foods he liked through her. She was aware of his presence and enjoyed having him with her. After the releasement process was complete and the therapist had gotten the husband into the Light, the wife decided she wanted to go back to her home. She agreed to go to the nursing home so she could be alone with her husband and to get away from those who thought she was crazy. Unfortunately, her children had put the house on the market and sold all her furniture. They did not know how to tell her or how she would react, so they asked the therapist if he would tell her. He did and her reaction was for them to take the house off the market (it had not sold at that point) and she would buy new furniture. It turned out to be a happy ending for everyone.

The Deceased Individual Wants to be Near a Loved One

Even if you do not ask a loved one to stay with you, they may want to. Again, they may not have an intention of attaching, but if the entity tried to "hug" or get too close to you, that would create a joining of your energies, such as the case of Whitney Houston hugging her daughter, Bobbi Kristina, after her passing. During this act of affection, Whitney became an attachment to her daughter, but that was not her intention. (More details on this situation in Part V.)

Possibly You Made An Unconscious Agreement With Them

This sometimes happens when two people express their love for each other and promise to always be together no matter what happens. It could also happen with a close friend or relative who passes.

Some Individuals Act as a Magnet to Earthbound Entities

If a person is vulnerable to attachments, the entity can attach while the host is unconscious/asleep, during surgery or a traumatic event, while intoxicated with drugs/alcohol, under extreme anger or stress, exhaustion, grief, fear or guilt. Sometimes the workplace houses many earthbound entities and we can take them home with us at the end of the day. Also, when we first begin to communicate with Spirit, it would be beneficial to make sure our energy is at a high vibration, that we protect ourselves, and make sure our Spiritual Guidance from the Light is with us to ensure that the earthbound entities are not the ones giving us answers to the advice we are seeking. If we open ourselves to anyone for communication purposes during meditation, we could attract an earthbound entity into our vibration. Then a releasement process would be necessary. It is a very common occurrence.

Important: Attachments can invade a physical body any time from conception to death. However, the attachment cannot take over the physical body if it chooses to join during the conception phase. When a soul is assigned a physical body and has a contract/blueprint for a physical life, an attachment CAN-NOT replace the incoming soul.

Chapter 8

SOME SIGNS WHICH MAY INDICATE AN ATTACHMENT IS PRESENT

Many times when I do a Soul Releasement session, the client will ask "How Do I Know When I Have an Attachment?" Below I have listed some of the most common indicators:

BEHAVIOR CHANGE

You start thinking and/or acting in a negative or destructive way which is not normal for you. You may experience anger, depression and even thoughts of suicide for no apparent reason.

Example: A mother consulted me regarding her five year old son. He was a very good boy, but occasionally he would act up and become violent and do destructive things. Later he would be sorry and tell his mommy that he did not know why he did what he did. In checking with my Spiritual Guidance, there was an earthbound boy who had been killed while playing outdoors on the property where this five year old now resided. This entity was ten years old when he died and was having fun playing with the five year old and getting him into trouble by making him do some naughty things. He was attached to the five year old and causing trouble, but when the younger boy was being punished for being bad, the attachment released itself. This is definitely not the type of invisible friend anyone needs.

FEARS OR PHOBIAS AND PANIC OR ANXIETY ATTACKS

If you develop fears or phobias or experience panic or anxiety attacks for no apparent reason, these conditions could be caused by an attachment(s).

SUDDEN CRAVINGS OR ADDICTIONS

If the attachment was addicted to any substance or had certain habits, these could be inflicted upon the host. These addictions/cravings are many; however, some of the most common ones are: drugs (both street and prescription), alcohol, food/ sugar/salt, sex, shopping -- anything that you become obsessive about.

TASTE IN CLOTHING STYLE/COLORS

This may be a personal desire on your part to make a change in your wardrobe, but if you make these changes and are wondering why you purchased something so hideous, "you" may not have been the one who made the choice. This can also pertain to changes in hair style/color.

RELATIONSHIPS CHANGE

If you start to experience problems in your relationships,

an attachment may be at the root cause. Many times attachments are the cause of relationship disturbances and/or breakups. Before consulting a divorce lawyer, you might want to make sure neither of you have attachments creating unnecessary problems.

HEARING VOICES

If you are open to connecting with Spirit, the attachments may try to communicate with you. It is important to make sure you ask your Spirit Guides if the voices you are hearing are coming from Light Beings or the earthbound or attached entities.

MULTIPLE PERSONALITIES

Occasionally, if you are hosting more than one entity, the different personalities of the attachments will surface through you.

LOSS OF MEMORY OR CONCENTRATION

While this is a common condition for many of us due to aging, too much stress, or going through the Ascension Process, attachment(s) who passed as a result of a traumatic accident or event, could cause you to experience temporary memory loss and foggy thinking.

PHYSICAL CONDITIONS

Ailments may appear without cause. Something as minor as a slight limp when you walk to an illness severe as cancer may appear if an attachment is present. A limp may show up immediately without cause; however, the attachment would have to be with you for quite some time in order for cancer to be diagnosed in your physical body. Migraine Headaches are a common cause if the attachment died as a result of a head injury. It's all about vibration.

Attachments can cause a great deal of havoc in our lives if we are not aware that they are with us. Checking with your Spirit Guides each day to make sure you are not carrying anyone else's energy should become a habit, such as taking a shower and brushing your teeth.

Chapter 9

THE EFFECTS OF AN ATTACHMENT TO YOUR ENERGY

The effects can range from as mild as "nesting" in your auric field, which would cause a drain of your energy level, to as severe as a full possession where you lose control of your life entirely, as the entity is very powerful and makes you do whatever it wants to do. This may be rare, but many times an attachment does cause the host to do things they would not normally do. The most extreme case would be if the attachment caused the death of the host.

In most cases when an individual commits suicide, their soul will remain on Earth as they are afraid that they might go to hell. However, the vibration of the attachment who committed suicide might be strong enough to cause the host to commit suicide when they would not have considered that action on their own.

Attachments can cause an individual to form a habit and usually it's not a "good" habit. Once the entity is released it will be necessary for the host to take the necessary steps in order to break the habit.

Attachments have the ability to hinder the host's spiritual growth by weighing down the host's energy and possibly causing the host to do or say things which are unkind, causing karma on a spiritual level and enemies on a physical level for the host.

Unfortunately, after physical death there is no possibility of spiritual growth as a result of the entity staying earthbound. There is a possibility that both the host and the attachment may each learn something, such as the host realizing that it needs to scan regularly for attachments in order to reach its full potential during physical existence. Many times attachments prevent us from growth by causing us to do what they want to do. If there are issues that need to be resolved, there is little or no possibility for this to happen. The lesson for the earthbound may be there is nothing to "fear" by returning to the Other Side after physical death. Fear is the main reason souls decide to stay on Earth after physical death.

Soul fragments of another human's soul can also attach to our energy field. Depending upon the traumatic nature of the individual's experience, the energy is usually very negative as a result of the anger, rage or stressful vibration the individual felt when their energy was directed at us. This is one situation where forgiveness is ultra important in releasing the energy to be returned to its rightful owner.

Can Attachments Release Themselves?

Absolutely! Attachments can and many times do release themselves from our energy. They do it all the time when they no longer feel comfortable in our energy field. Therefore, if circumstances happen in your life that change your vibration (if you are too scattered, which lowers your vibration, or too calm which raises your vibration), they will release themselves and find another host who is more compatible with their energy.

I attended a meditation class in New York City many years ago. First, in order to release any stress we were carrying, the instructor had us lay on the floor and kick, scream, roll and thrash around. I laughed so hard during this exercise thinking that if someone entered the room late for this class, they would think we had all lost our minds. The room was in complete darkness (no windows in the room) even though it was early afternoon. At one point I opened my eyes and saw that the ceiling was filled with little sparks of light like twinkling stars in the nighttime sky. I was in the early stages of my spiritual path and very curious about everything, but did not have the knowledge I now have regarding earthbound entities. Those little twinkling stars were entities that had been released from the attendees as a result of all the commotion during the stress release exercise. Had I realized that then, I would have called in my Spirit Guides to assist those souls to the Light or I could have created a portal as a passageway for them.

Chapter 10

THREE VERY IMPORTANT THINGS WE CAN DO TO BE FREE OF ATTACHMENTS

The three things I consider most important in keeping ourselves free of attachments are to:

1 Keep our vibration at the highest level possible

2. Protect our energy DAILY.

3. Connect/Communicate with our Spirit Guides

HOW TO INCREASE YOUR LEVEL OF VIBRATION

It is important to work daily on keeping your energy vibration as high as possible. High vibration is our insurance policy to be free of attachments. Remember like attracts like energy and the higher your energy, the less likely you will attract an earthbound entity. Some suggestions for doing this would be:

Prayer/Meditation

Deep Breathing

Breathing in Colors – Red/Gold/Platinum

Positive Thinking

Healthy Diet & Proper Exercise

Proper Amount of Sleep/Rest

Drink Plenty of Water to Assist in Detoxifying the Body

Laughter

Listen to Classical, Uplifting, Easy Listening Music

VISUALIZATION EXERCISES TO INCREASE YOUR VIBRATION

- Before going to bed each night, in a meditative state, mentally ask that any of your own energy which may have left your energy field throughout the day return to you. And DEMAND that any energy which is NOT your own release itself from your energy field. Attachments also have Free Will so you cannot demand that they go to the Light, but you can demand that they leave your energy field. You can ask your Spirit Guides to be with you during this time to ensure that what you are requesting happens.

- As a visualization exercise, daily mentally bring liquid Golden/White Light in through your crown chakra and bathe your entire inner and outer bodies with it. This is the God/Christ Light, which will bring your energy to a higher level.

- In meditation ask your Higher God Self, the Angels, Spirit Guides, and Ascended Masters (those who have been assigned to watch over you during your earthly journey) to be sure you are free of attachments. We need to do this daily. We cannot issue a blanket request for the rest of our life. The reason is Free Will. Our Angelic Guidance would be interfering with our Free Will by not allowing us to make choices on a daily basis.

IMPORTANCE OF PROTECTION

Individuals who communicate with the Spirit World should always make sure that they protect themselves. Bring the Golden/White Light down from the 9th dimension and wrap it around your entire inner and outer bodies. Then say a prayer. Any prayer you are comfortable with is fine. You can even make up your own, which many individuals do. Or follow whatever protection procedure you have already established or feel comfortable with.

CONNECTING & COMMUNICATING WITH YOUR SPIRIT GUIDES

Our Heavenly Helpers are assigned to us to help guide us through our life challenges and lessons. If your vibration is low do not think that by connecting with your Angels, Spirit Guides, Ascended Masters, or your Higher Self, that these Light Beings will raise your vibration. The Light Beings can lower their vibration to a certain point in order to assist us; however, it is much easier for them if we raise our vibration. The higher our vibration, the higher level Light Beings we are able to con-nect with.

We need to take steps to increase our rate of vibration and then connect with our guidance. When our vibration is low, we attract the lower vibrating entities. It is also extremely important that we always indicate that our intention is to connect with our Angels, Spirit Guides, Ascended Masters, Higher Self, etc., from the Light. Therefore, earthbound entities will not be able to attach to our energy. Guidance from the Light would NEVER attach to our energy or try to control our thoughts or actions. They are very loving, protective beings who are only interested in assisting us if we ASK them. That is how they attain spiritual growth on the Other Side – by assisting us on Earth with our challenges.

One of the things they can help us with is to keep us informed if we are carrying any energy that is NOT our own. However, I can guarantee that they are capable of so much more. If you are not already communicating with your Spirit Guides, try using this very simple visualization exercise:

Imagine yourself in a very safe and comfortable setting – by a beach, stream, brook, lake or ocean, in a forest, or the desert – wherever you feel peaceful and calm. Take a few deep breaths and let them out forcefully to release any stress you may be holding onto. Focus your attention upward and view the beautiful blue sky and white puffy clouds. Then pick up the nearby telephone and ask to speak to your Angels, Spirit Guides, or Higher Self. You do not have to dial any numbers (there is no 800 number or extension to worry about). Then have your conversation. Ask any questions you want. If you don't "think" you received a response, they will somehow get your answer to you, through a dream, another person or something you see in a magazine or on TV or possibly hear on the radio. The important thing for you to do is relax and ASK.

BREAKING A HABIT ACQUIRED FROM AN ATTACHMENT

If you acquire a habit from an attached entity, depending upon the length of time they were with you, you may have to take conscious steps in order to break the habit. However, if the entity was with you for a very short period of time, the habit may automatically disappear as soon as the entity is released. Repetition causes a habit to be formed; however, it takes a lot of concentrated effort to break a habit. Sudden weight gain may be the cause of an attachment. After releasement of the entity, you would have to take conscious steps to release the weight.

A college student was doing quite well, then, suddenly became suicidal. This individual was a relative of a friend of mine. I had performed releasement work on my friend so she asked if I could help her cousin. It was discovered that her cousin had attachments. Once the entities were released, she returned to her normal life/self. The attachments which caused thoughts of suicide were with the host only a short period of time so it was easy for the host to return to normalcy once the attachments were released. Recently I received word from my friend that her cousin was still doing fine.

Another lady was very upset and actually suicidal over the passing of her mother-in-law. While they had a good relationship, it seemed highly unusual for an individual to want to commit suicide as a result of their mother-in-law's passing, no matter how good the relationship was. (I'm a mother-in-law so I am not making jokes here). The lady was admitted to the psychiatric ward of a local hospital. When she was released she looked absolutely terrible. I checked her for attachments, knowing that a hospital was an excellent place to pick some up, and discovered she had 40 entities attached to her.

Some of them joined her while she was in the hospital, but the suicidal thoughts came as a result of entities that had committed suicide and attached to her energy field prior to her mother-in-law's death. She may have also acquired some of these attachments during the wake and funeral services of her mother-in-law. The death triggered their desire not to want to be here and, because they were attachments, their thoughts became her thoughts. It took a great deal of time to convince the 40 attachments to release from her energy field and to be escorted to the Light. After the releasement she did not commit suicide; however she needed to seek professional counseling.

Many times when a soul (or a soul fragment) attaches to another human's energy field it is by accident. Once connected with the energy field of a living breathing human, the non-physical being realizes they can continue to "live" through another and depending upon how strong the attachment's energy, they can take full control of the thoughts, words, actions and feelings of the host's body. Many times the attached energy just resides in the auric field and goes with the flow. This is called "nesting." While they may not be causing the host any discomfort, they are causing the host's energy level to be lower than it would be if they did not occupy space.

Chapter 11

SOME HELPFUL HINTS BEFORE YOU BEGIN THE SOUL RELEASEMENT PROCEDURE

At one point in my Soul Releasement work, the only thing that was important was to release the entity from the host. It didn't take me long to discover that just releasing them was NOT enough as most likely they would return in a short period of time and re-attach to the same host or find another suitable host to attach to. So the problem was not really being addressed fully.

ESCORT FROM THE LIGHT

In the Soul Releasement Procedure, it is important to have an escort from the Light available to take the released soul(s) to wherever they are supposed to be as they cannot get there on their own. If you just release their energy from the host they have attached to, they will either return shortly or find another unsuspecting host. They need an escort from the Light to take them where they need to be as they are not able to get there without an escort. Many times it may be necessary for them to go to the Resting Area for restoration of their soul energy before being admitted into the Light (aka Heaven). Trust that the Spirit Guides will KNOW exactly where the soul(s) needs to be. ALL souls need an escort upon death to bring them to the higher dimensions.

Importance of a Leader & a Scout for Multiple Attachments

If two or more entities attach to one individual, the entity with the strongest, more aggressive personality will assume the role of "leader"; that is the entity you want to communicate with when attempting to release their energy from the host. Many times the "leader" will not want to be released, but some of the others are willing to go to the higher dimensions. In this case, ask that those who are willing to be escorted by a Light Being for the purpose of viewing where they will go and then returning with the Light Being to the host so that the "scout" can relay what they experienced on the Other Side to the "leader" and any attachments who stayed behind. This will usually convince the others to join the "scout" upon their return to the Other Side. This is a technique that my Spiritual Guidance provided to me when during my counseling work I was having difficulty convincing entities to leave.

Attachments May Try to Deceive You

NEVER trust the "word" of the attachment that they will leave. They cannot be trusted as they want you to go away and leave them alone. If they do leave, it is momentarily and then they will return when you are no longer working with the host's energy field. Your Spirit Guides will act as their escort to ensure a safe arrival.

Unresolved Issues of the Attachment Will be Dealt With on the Other Side

DO NOT try to "fix" the problems of the attachment. The important thing is to release them from the host's energy field and into the higher dimension through an escort. If there is anything that needs fixing, that can be done on the Other Side. The important thing for you to do regarding the attachment is to inform them of the importance of forgiveness of those who have hurt them, as well as self-forgiveness. However, you will need to work with your client in cleansing their energy field from the negative energy the attachment has left behind. The cleansing process is covered separately in this section as well as in Item No. 11 in the releasement procedure.

Host Does Not Want the Attachment Released

If the host (human) indicates that they do not want the entity released from their energy (this may happen if they discover that the attachment is a deceased loved one), that does not mean that you have to leave it. The attached entity has Free Will and if they want to be released and escorted to the Other Side, that is the deciding factor. This is why it is important to always work with the Beings of Light as they will be able to assist an attachment in leaving even if the host does not want to let them go. In this type of situation, I would not argue with the client, but I would work remotely (at a distance in meditation) with the host's Higher Self and my Spirit Guides to release the entity to the Light.

Entity Refuses to Leave

On the other hand, if the entity refuses to leave the Earth plane, under spiritual law, they have Free Will to stay, BUT only as an earthbound entity – NOT as an attachment. Archangel Michael demonstrated this piece of the counseling session when I was conducting an evening meditation class at a business establishment in my local area. There were several earthbound entities of a very negative nature at this location. Archangel Michael assisted me in releasing them while the group of ladies was meditating.

Afterwards, Archangel Michael indicated that there was only one entity that refused to go with him to the Light. Archangel Michael instructed the entity that it could stay, but it would not be able to enter the premises or attach to anyone's energy field. I did not share this information with anyone in the group. However, the next week before class started, one of the ladies went to the storage area in the back of the building. She let out an unbelievable loud and long scream. We all went rushing to see what the problem was. She said that she saw a pair of eyes (only eyes) looking at her from outside the building. The entity followed Archangel Michael's instructions by not coming into the building. I did connect with the entity again that evening and told him he could not look in the windows either and it would be best if he found another location to reside.

Attachments are not part of our Soul Contract, and once the attachments are discovered we can then enforce spiritual law by not allowing them to take up residence in our energy field or in our locations.

ATTACHMENT TO ASK HOST FOR FORGIVENESS

It is important in the counseling session with the attachment to have them ask the host for forgiveness for any problems they may have caused in the host's life. If this is not possible at the time of releasement, it will be possible once they get to the Other Side and are able to see the error of their ways during the Life Review session. They will want to be forgiven and will find a way of getting word to the host even if it has to be through the host's Higher Self and not on a conscious level. Also, it would be appropriate to ask the host to extend forgiveness to the entity as a precautionary measure in clearing the connection.

WORKING WITH THE HOST'S HIGHER SELF

In addition to working with my Spirit Guides, I sometimes work with the Higher Self of the host, as I did in the case of Whitney Houston (detailed in Part V). Even if you are working with the Higher Self, you still need your Spirit Guides to assist the attachment(s) to the Light. Ask your Spirit Guides if the person you are scheduled to work with is carrying any energy that is not their own? If you receive a "Yes" response, it is time to connect with their Higher Self.

Mentally call out to the person's Higher Self. Identify yourself and your intention to release energy from the human that is not their own and is interfering with the life plan of the host. The Higher Self is our protector and will not allow you to do anything to harm the individual. Sometimes it takes a while to connect with the Higher Self and other times the connection is immediate. I'm not sure why this is. It helps to state your intention as that is what is important. It is not important who you are, just that you mean no harm. The Higher Self can tell you how many attachments there are, what their gender is and what area of the host's body the attachments are located, as well as any other information you may need to complete your work. I like to know where the entities are located so that I can make sure those areas receive extra Light energy during the cleansing process after the entities are released. Also, when you report the area(s) where the entities were located, the host many times reports that they have had physical issues in those areas.

For those occasions when I am not able to connect with the Higher Self of the individual I am working with, my Spiritual Guidance will make the connection for me. Then I can go forward with the Releasement Process with the help of the Higher Self to provide information as to how many entities are attached, where they are located within the energy field and confirming when they have been released so that I can begin the clearing of any negative energy which may be left in the individual's auric field.

THE CLEANSING PROCESS

The cleansing process is a visualization exercise as follows: Imagine that liquid golden white Light is being downloaded from the higher dimensions into the host's crown chakra, and the Light slowly and gently expands to encompass the inner and outer bodies (physical body as well as the auric field). The intention is that liquid Light is more powerful. I imagine it to be the consistency of Wite-Out ™, the correction fluid. If I know where the entities resided on or in the host, I will add an extra amount of the liquid golden white Light to those areas to ensure that all the negativity is absorbed. Then I bring the liquid golden white Light out through the bottom of the host's feet and deposit it into Mother Earth for further cleansing if necessary. Next I ask that a shower of golden white Light, from the 9th dimension, be wrapped around the energy of the host like a cocoon or blanket to further assist in the healing process.

WORKING IN THE HOST'S BEST INTEREST

When working with a client, it may be best not to mention the Soul Releasement work. You might want to ask for their permission in releasing old negative energies or in doing some emotional or auric clearing work. Many times the attachment(s) will do everything in their power to dissuade the process from happening as they are comfortable and don't want to leave. Work with the individual's Higher Self for permission to do the Soul Releasement work and also to know how many (if any) attachments there are is all that is necessary. You do not have to obtain permission from the host on a conscious level. The Higher Self is our gatekeeper and will not allow anyone to do anything that is not appropriate or in their highest best interest.

Usually the host is totally unaware that they are carrying attachments. The thoughts, desires and actions of the attachments are experienced through the host as if they were that of the host. Even if the host thinks or says that they can't believe they did or said something, it is perceived by themselves as well as others that it was the sole desires, thoughts, words or actions of the physical being. If an entity is attached for quite some time, the thoughts, feelings, words and actions (whether positive or negative) become a habit for the host. Even after the attachment is released, the host will have to work hard to break any bad habits created by the attachments. If the entity is released within a relatively short period of time after its attachment, it usually doesn't have enough time to create a bad habit and the host returns to its normal thoughts, feelings, words and actions immediately.

SOUL RELEASEMENT -- CANCELLATIONS

If you are scheduled to do work with a client or group to assist in releasing energy from them that is not their own, be prepared for cancellations. The attached energies will cause this effect as they will want to keep things at the status quo.

I had a group meeting scheduled to talk about the releasement process and do a group releasement exercise. There are always some legitimate cancellations; however, one woman ended up coming in late. Very apologetic she explained all the things that happened – her car wouldn't start. She borrowed a friend's car so she could make the class. Then a long-time friend that she hadn't seen in years paid her a surprise visit.

But she was determined to be at the meeting as she "knew" there was someone or something interfering with her life and she wanted to get rid of it. The process was successful for her and I admired her determination to fix her life.

Depending upon how many or the strength of their vibration, it is not easy to override the attachment(s)'s wishes. We have to be more determined to release them as it is our life and they are interfering.

It is when I work with clients without their conscious knowledge (I work with their Higher Self) that the success happens more easily.

Chapter 12

PROCEDURE TO CONNECT WITH AND RELEASE ATTACHMENTS

Following is the spiritual procedure I have been guided to use in a Soul Releasement session:

PROCEDURE TO CONNECT WITH & RELEASE ATTACHMENTS

1. Always PROTECT yourself. I use the Golden/White Light. Mentally bring down a combination of Golden/White Light from the 9th dimension and wrap it around your inner and outer bodies for the purpose of protecting yourself from any negative or earthbound energy attaching to you while doing releasement work.

2. Call upon your Heavenly Helpers – Angels, Spirit Guides, Ascended Masters and Higher (God) Self and/or Jesus/Sananda and Archangel Michael or any of the Light Beings you may be working with. You will need someone from the Light to be an escort for the released souls, as they cannot get to where they need to be on their own.

3. As an additional precaution, ask your Heavenly Helpers to ensure that you are free of attached entities and protected from the entities to be released from attaching to your energy.

4. Ask your Heavenly Helpers if there are any earthbound entities attached to the person you are working with, and, if so, how many and where they are located on the host? Entities can attach to your aura field and/or anywhere on or within our body they feel comfortable. When I know this information, I add extra Light to those areas during the cleansing process to ensure that any negative energy is absorbed. Light is the best cleansing agent for negativity.

5. If "Yes", mentally/telepathically start talking with the attachment(s). Tell them if they have questions, you will be happy to answer them. However, your purpose is to provide passage to the Light for them.

6. Don't be surprised if you don't get a response even though you KNOW that they are there. If there is more than one entity ask to speak to the strongest (most powerful) one -- the one who will act as the leader for the group. Usually one will be the spokesman for them all. If there is only one, just keep talking until you get a response from the entity. This is the start of your counseling session.

7. Usually I am guided by my Heavenly Helpers as to what I say, but some of the standard comments are:

- Assure them that your only purpose is to help them return to the Other Side where they need to be. Being on Earth without a physical body is as close to hell as they are going to get. They are "stuck" in the vibration they were in at the time of death. If it was a traumatic passing, they will relive that experience over and over again. Definitely not worth it.

- Tell them there is a better, much better, place for them to be now. They will be able to view their loved ones on Earth from this better place once they are situated.

- No matter what they did while in physical form, God automatically forgives them. God views our wrong-doings as experiences which can be corrected at another time. They need to forgive themselves and anyone who has hurt them. No matter what anyone has done, it is no longer important and they will know this as fact when they return to the higher realms.

- Tell them that some of the world's worst dictators made it to Heaven so they will have no problem.

- Tell them that the only contraband not allowed in Heaven is negative energy. Encourage them to release and let go of any negative energy they accumulated at the soul level on Earth, and this will bring their energy to a higher vibration and make their transition from Earth to Spirit much easier.

- If they continue to hold onto the negativity, they will be brought to the Resting Area. This is not a bad or evil place. It is a place for the soul to be restored and this can be done through the vibrations of Love, Forgiveness & Compassion.

- There is a possibility that your counseling efforts will be ignored. In that case, if there is only one entity, tell it that an escort will take it to the Other Side and show it around with a guarantee that, if it is not happy, the escort will bring it back to Earth. However, if it chooses to return to Earth, it will not be able to reattach to the host or any other human. If there are a group of attached souls, ask one or two to volunteer to go with the escort to view the Other Side and then return with the escort to share with the others what they witnessed. Almost 100% of the time when the entity returns and is excited about where they went and want to go back, the others will follow. In all the years I have been doing this work, only one time did an entity return to Earth, but promised to go back once they resolved an issue (forgiveness) they thought could only be resolved on earth.

- Remind them that Earth is a physical planet and we need a physical body while here. Once the physical body dies there is no purpose and no further growth for them by remaining on Earth.

8. Ask the attachment to request forgiveness from the host for any harm they may have caused during their stay. If they are not ready for this, it can be done from the Other Side. Also ask the host to express forgiveness to the attachment before their departure. This will make the transition much easier.

9. Your Heavenly Helpers will let you know when the entity/entities agree to go. At that point you can bid them good-bye or say any parting words that you feel are necessary.

10. If, for any reason, the entity refuses to leave, you need to instruct them that they have Free Will and can stay on Earth, however, they absolutely must detach from the host and not reattach to the host or any other human. To continue to cling to the host's energy would be a violation of the host's Free Will, and this will not be tolerated. Your Heavenly Helpers will be able to provide further instruction to the attachment(s), if necessary, regarding spiritual laws they are violating.

11. After the attachment(s) are gone, ask that a thick shower of liquid golden white Light from the 9th dimension come into the client's crown chakra (top of head) and slowly and gently trickle down throughout their inner and outer bodies absorbing any negative energy left behind by the attachment(s) all the way down to the bottom of their feet. This is a

cleansing process to make sure any residue from the attachment(s) is cleaned up.

Keep in mind the above procedure is a general outline of what I do in a session. Each practitioner/therapist will adjust the releasement process to fit what works for them or as guided by their Spiritual (non-physical) Helpers. Trust your own Spirit Guides to know what's best in the particular situation you are dealing with at the time. Many times the attachment(s) are eager to leave because they have been waiting a long time for someone to rescue them, and it takes very little counseling on your part.

REMOTE RELEASEMENT

This is done at a distance through meditation. You do not have to work face-to-face with the individual. Ninety to ninety-five percent of my Soul Releasement work is done remotely. Connecting with the Higher Self of the person who believes they may have an attachment, and working with the client while they sleep to release any attachments is a method I have found to be very effective. It is most beneficial when the person with attachments (referred to as host) is not aware that the releasement is to take place. Many times when I discuss with a client that attachments are present and I will release them, the attachments cause the host to say he/she does not want to go forward with the session. It is not always necessary or appropriate to get the conscious consent of the host. When I do the work remotely, I work with the host's Higher Self. The Higher

Self is our gatekeeper and will not allow anything to happen to the host. I depend on the Higher Self to reveal if there are attachments, if so, how many, and where they are located on the physical body. Then I do not give up until they are released and escorted to the Light.

Chapter 13

PSYCHIC ATTACKS AND CURSES

A psychic attack is negative energy directed at you either verbally or through thoughts from another human still in physical form. It would be a good idea to check with your Heavenly Helpers regularly to see if you are carrying energy that belongs to someone else still in human form. If so, you can avoid this by releasing any energy you have accumulated throughout your day and ask that it be returned to its rightful owner accompanied (or surrounded) by God's (not your) Love and Light vibration. This will neutralize the negativity and, hopefully, bring peace to the originator of the negative energy. Trust your Heavenly Helpers to know whether you are experiencing a psychic attack by another human's verbal or thought forms or if the negativity is coming from a non-physical entity. Either way, your Spiritual Team will be able to assist you, if you ASK them.

The Powerful Tool of Forgiveness

FORGIVENESS is a powerful tool in the case of Psychic Attack as it is the negative thought formations directed at you from another individual who is upset with you that can cause harm without you even knowing why. If negative thoughts are continuously directed at you, they could eventually cause much pain and suffering on all levels – physically, mentally, emotionally and/or spiritually. Whether or not you know the individual(s) who directed negativity at you, it is in your highest best interest to follow the FORGIVENESS route, as it is the KEY to Heaven!

Are Curses Real?

They are if you "think" they are real. I had someone tell me that they were going to put a curse on me. They were upset with me for something I said that they didn't like. I just laughed and said that they might as well put it on themselves as that is where it would end up anyway. I do believe in "what goes around comes around." I'm not sure if they sent negative energy my way or not, but I don't believe in curses, so I do not fuel them with the fear vibration. Also, I am in the habit of protecting myself daily and in communication with my Spirit Guides daily as well.

I attended one of Dr. Larry Dossey's workshops, and he told the story about one of his patients who was in the process of dying for no apparent reason. It was not an attachment, but a curse that had been placed on his patient by another person. The patient believed the individual had the power to cause his death as a result of the curse. Dr. Dossey knew that this was not possible, however, no amount of medication was helping the patient get better. His vital signs were dropping quickly and, he would have died if Dr. Dossey did not do something quick. Dr. Dossey thought if the curse was causing his patient to experience the dying process, it might be possible to save his patient's life by removing the curse. He convinced another doctor at the hospital to assist him in a "ritual" to remove the curse from his patient. Neither doctor knew how to remove a curse, but they decided to use theatrics. One evening after hours at the hospital, the doctors wheeled the patient to an empty operating room. They told the patient that they were going to remove the curse and then he would be fine. They lit candles, chanted, and in a very demanding, authoritative manner verbally removed the curse. As they wheeled the patient back to his room, they told him to get a good night's sleep as he would be his old self in the morning. Guess what? The next morning his vital signs were normal. He was extremely hungry as he hadn't eaten in quite a few days and ate a huge breakfast. He was released from the hospital that morning after breakfast in perfect health.

One of my favorite sayings is: "Your thoughts create your reality!" This was certainly true for Dr. Dossey's patient. The patient believed that the doctor had stronger powers than the person who had placed the curse on him, so it was only natural that the doctor could remove it. Fear was also involved with this situation. Fear is an enemy. Do not let it get a hold of you. Trust, have faith and believe that if you protect yourself from harm and you are connected with your Spiritual Guidance, "darkness" does not have a chance of coming in.

Chapter 14

MEDICAL CONDITIONS OR ATTACHMENTS?

First of all, I am NOT a medical professional and I am not in a position to comment from a scientific or medical perspective. My reference here to medical conditions possibly stemming from an attachment is from a spiritual perspective only. I recommend that individuals seek medical help first and as an additional measure to check for attachments.

My experience in dealing with attachments is that the vibration of the attachment's energy at the time of death has a profound physical and/or psychological effect on the host.

As an example: A young lady attended one of my Connect with Your Angels Workshops. Several months later I received a call from her saying that her Angels told her to call me. She was experiencing debilitating heart problems to the point where she had to leave her job and was confined to a wheelchair (at age thirty-two). Unfortunately, her local doctor was not able to find any medical problems with his testing. Everything was perfect. He then made an appointment for her at a specialty hospital for more advanced testing.

She couldn't understand why her Angels wanted her to contact me because I wasn't a medical doctor. I told her I would meditate to see what was occurring even though I highly suspected that she had an attachment. Sure enough, upon checking with my Angels, it was revealed that her grandfather had died of a massive heart attack. His purpose for attaching to her was to protect her. However, the vibration of his energy attached to her energy caused her to experience the same symptoms which resulted in his death. He did not want to leave her until I told him that if he didn't detach from her, she would die just as he did and that wasn't fair to her. He did not want any harm to come to his granddaughter so he agreed to go.

When I called her the next day to report my findings, she knew exactly when "something" happened. She had been awakened as I was doing the releasement work, felt wonderful, and when she tried to get out of bed, she discovered she didn't need the wheelchair. She had complete mobility back. I told her she still needed to keep her appointment with the specialty hospital, and if she felt comfortable she could explain that she contacted a spiritualist who performed a releasement session, which brought her back to normal mobility. She was not comfortable with trying to explain this to the doctors and just accepted her clean bill of health that everything was fine.

There are two possible reasons why her local doctor was not able to diagnose what she was experiencing:

1. The entity detached from her energy during the doctor's visit.

2. While the patient was experiencing the actual symptoms through her grandfather's energy vibration, these symptoms were not hers yet. The vibration had not been there long enough to create physical damage to her heart. Eventually she would have experienced the physical damage.

My hope is that someday the medical profession will feel comfortable working with the spiritual side of healing.

Dissociative Identity Disorder and Spirit Possession Syndrome

If a patient is diagnosed with DID, it would be in the patient's best interest to scan the body for attachments. If there are attachments, they need to be released immediately. The releasement process would assist the patient/host in its recovery sooner rather than later. Some of the symptoms of DID are identical to those which are caused by an attachment or possession.

Multiple Personality or Split Personality Disorder

The issues associated with the different personalities created need to be resolved and the personalities integrated with the original personality in order for the individual to be healed or freed from the condition. However, if the different personalities are not of the patient, but caused by multiple attachments, the releasement process could speed up the patient's recovery.

Schizophrenia

Another condition which may be caused by soul attachments is schizophrenia. The voices the patient is hearing may be those of an attachment(s). Again, it would be in the patient's highest interest to scan for attachments. If entities are found they would also be classified as Possessions.

Please note: These medical disorders are severe enough so that Soul/Spirit Releasement Therapy, should be considered in addition to medical and psychological treatments. If entities are attached to patients with the above disorders, they would be classified as Possessions!

TRANSVESTITES & TRANSEXUALS

It is very possible that a female possession may be responsible for a physical male to have the desire to be a female, or for a male possession to create the feelings in a physical female to be a male. It would be advisable to scan for possessions before scheduling surgery to make sure that a "mistake" is not made. If an attachment is superimposing these desires onto a host, there is definitely karma being created and a very uncomfortable lifestyle for the unsuspecting human. Once the energy of the attachment is cleared, the host may feel very differently regarding their preferences and decide not to have the sex change surgery. If attachments are the cause of the desire to make a sex change, they would also be classified as Possessions.

FALSE MEMORIES

Sometimes during a hypnosis session, men who served in the armed forces during wartime would recall being killed in battle when in fact they did not die. One thought might be that they had served in a different war in a past life and in that lifetime they were killed. However, if the hypnosis subject had entities attached, it could be that it was the attached entity's memories that were surfacing during the session not those of the subject.

Example: I was working with a client who "thought" she was sexually abused at a very early age in this lifetime. In checking with my Spirit Guides it was revealed that she had this experience in a past life, brought it forward to resolve in this lifetime through the Life Lesson of forgiveness. Instead, she held onto the anger as if it had happened in this lifetime. These false memories have literally haunted her and have interfered with her being able to live a happy and productive life. Hopefully, she will come to the realization that it does not matter, who, why, when it happened. Letting it go through forgiveness is the answer to her problems.

ENTITY ATTACHMENTS

There are many medical conditions which may be caused by attachments or possessions. Therefore, I encourage every individual to be responsible for making sure that you are free of any energy that is not your own. The sooner you are able to release them, the better life will be for you and them as well because they will be in a much better place and you can go forward and live your own life as you want to.

Chapter 15

Suicide Victims

It's almost a guarantee that individuals who commit
suicide will stay earthbound. Many times they are afraid that
they will go to "hell" so they stay where they are familiar. Upon
learning of the death of a relative through suicide, I knew
his soul would be earthbound so I immediately sat down to
meditate and called in my Spirit Guides to assist me in guiding
his soul to the Light. I was very surprised by my Spirit Guide's
reaction – an absolute NO! He needed time to adjust to his
circumstances.

He was filled with hate and anger, severe depression and
many other negative qualities. If I reached out to connect with
his energy at that time, there was a possibility that he would
have become a possession to my energy – not an attachment.
Calling out to him so soon after his death might have been
considered an invitation for him to join me. He was definitely
not ready to go to the Light at that time.

It took years of Earth time before he was ready and I assisted him at that time. I thank my guides for directing me away from doing this work when I was so eager to assist. This is why it is ultra important to call in your Spiritual Guidance before connecting with the souls of any earthbound entity and to allow your guidance to lead you as they know all circumstances and what is in the highest best interest of all. It may not be the proper time or it may not be your spiritual responsibility to work with that particular soul. Our guidance knows what our plan calls for so we need to trust them.

Chapter 16

WHEN THE HOST OF AN ATTACHMENT DIES

Following are a few possibilities of what might happen upon the death of a host:

1. If the attachment is weak and only nesting or hiding, it can go to the Light along with the soul of the deceased host.

2. If the attachment is more powerful than the host, it could anchor the deceased human to stay earthbound.

3. The attachment could dislodge its energy from the host and move on to find another host allowing the deceased human host to go to the Light as is natural.

4. Or it could stay earthbound, wait for its host to return in another physical incarnation and re-attach at that point, possibly for revenge purposes or to be connected with a loved one, but was afraid to go to the Light when they had an opportunity.

5. Unfortunately, rarely there is only one attachment to a host. If many earthbound entities are attached, their combined negative energy could anchor the deceased host to remain earthbound with them. When the attachment(s) continues to cling to the recently deceased soul, keeping it earthbound, this is referred to as the piggyback effect.

6. They could detach from each other and go their separate ways or they could cluster together (the piggyback effect) which would make them more powerful and able to actually possess another human host.

Chapter 17

DEMONIC-TYPE ENTITIES AND MY SECRET WEAPON

Personally, I do not believe in the "devil" or demonic entities. I only believe in positive and negative energy. Those souls who have had a rough or abusive life and carry a lot of anger, rage, revenge or resentment are perceived as demonic in nature. If they do exist, I have been very fortunate not to have had contact with them.

Many years ago when I was in training to become a minister, I was counseling a lady who was experiencing quite a bit of turmoil in her life. Because I already had the knowledge of doing Soul Releasement work, my guides gave me a heads up that this individual was carrying a very negative earthbound entity, which was compounding her problems. At that time I thought it was necessary to get her permission to do the releasement work. Of course she refused, stating she didn't believe that was her problem (the attachment caused her to say that). This is very common when you try to get the host's permission on a conscious level.

For many years this lady continued to suffer as a result of the entity attached to her energy field. I happened to be presenting a class on the Soul's Mission (it had nothing to do with Soul Releasement), which she was attending. Before class she mentioned that someone had told her that she had a dark entity around her that was causing her harm. I told her all she had to do was call in Archangel Michael or Jesus, tell the entity it was not welcome and it needed to leave. If it refused to leave, Archangel Michael and/or Jesus would see to it that it did. Shortly after class began, this nice lady apologized for interrupting, but the entity was causing severe pain in her stomach (solar plexus) area and she could hardly stand it. I closed my eyes and took a moment of silence to check if it was the attached entity causing her pain.

I knew that Jesus and Archangel Michael were with me during my lecture and they confirmed it was. So I told the entity to get the "hell" out of there as it was disrupting my class. When I opened my eyes she said "What did you do? The pain is gone." I replied, "I did what I told you to do," and went back to lecturing.

This was a perfect demonstration of how easy releasement work is. I was confident that Jesus/Sananda and Archangel Michael were with me for the lecture and that they would take care of seeing this entity to the Light or making sure that it did not return to the host. You just have to be firm and let them know you mean business.

Fear is a powerful source of fuel for the deceased entity to use and, you can be assured that they will take advantage and use that power. Know that you are protected, your Heavenly Helpers are with you and that no harm will come to you. I am usually more gentle with my releasement work, but I think my Heavenly Helpers felt this entity needed to be dealt with in an aggressive manner.

MY "SECRET" WEAPON -- THE ARCTURIANS!

If you have occasion to work with the more difficult (demonic-type) entities, call upon the Arcturians. They are very high level, non-physical, Light Beings assigned by God to humanity. I called upon them frequently when I was suffering with a great deal of pain. However, when I was not able to assist an individual in releasing a very negative attachment, my Spiritual Team guided me to call upon the Arcturians for assistance.

During meditation I call upon the Arcturians to please come forward -- I need their help. I give them whatever information I have regarding the individual/host needing their assistance. This information would consist of their name, address, city, state, country, age. Finally, I ask them to check out the situation, do what they can to release the attachment(s) and to report back to me the outcome so I can pass word on to the client.

I don't call upon the Arcturians often, but they are a true Godsend when I need them. Be patient. Sometimes it may take a while before the Arcturians return to you with information. At any rate, you can be confident if you turned the releasement process over to the Arcturians. I am sure they have their own method, but they have not shared it with me at this point.

I had a client who scheduled a reading with me regarding some situations going on in his life that he didn't understand. His wife was his primary concern. They met, fell in love, got married and enjoyed life together for only a short period of time before things went awry. She had attempted suicide and was currently in the hospital. He said that she had not been depressed, and she did not have a history of depression or suicide genetically. My guidance indicated that her attempt had been the result of attachment activity. I worked with my Spirit Guides (in this case the Arcturians) in the releasement process. They watched over her even after the releasement as her energy was very vulnerable for additional entities to attach to. My guides indicated that it would be 4 or 5 months before she would be restored to normal functioning as a result of the damage caused by the attached entities. While this may appear to be demonic in nature, it resulted because several of the many attached entities had committed suicide and the others were at an extremely low vibration due to circumstances in their life while in physical form.

Again, I cannot praise the Arcturians highly enough. They helped me when I was in severe pain and now they are assisting in getting the most difficult souls into the Light. God called upon them to help humanity during our transitional phase of rising into the higher dimensions, so do not be afraid to call upon them for help.

PART III

ASSISTING SOULS FROM THE RESTING AREA INTO THE LIGHT

Chapter 18

WHAT IS THE RESTING AREA?

The Catholics refer to this area as "purgatory." The Tibetan Buddhists refer to it as the "bardo." However, in my conversations with Jesus/Sananda, He refers to it as – the Resting Area, the Gray Level, or the basement level of Heaven. I prefer to use "The Resting Area." In my opinion, it is an accurate description – a place for the Soul to rest after a challenging physical life.

No matter what you call it, this is an area where souls go as a result of a traumatic/unexpected passing or a very challenging life who did not release their negativity on the Earth plane. It is not a bad or evil place. It is a place for the soul to release and let go of the negative energy they accumulated while on Earth in their own time with the help of Angels, Spirit Guides and sometimes human assistance from the Earth plane. There is beautiful music and colors that we can't even imagine which assist with the soul's healing process. Souls can bypass the Resting Area through their spiritual growth while on Earth. Releasing your earthly problems through the vibrations of Love, Forgiveness and Compassion is an important step to being admitted to the higher dimensions immediately upon passing.

My Father as the First Soul I Counseled

After I had been assisting earthbound and attached souls to the Other Side for a few years, Jesus and Archangel Michael asked me to work with them in counseling souls in the Resting Area so that they could be admitted to the Light (Heaven). I was surprised that my father was the first soul I counseled. I wasn't really sure how to do this work so I had to learn through trial and error.

One of the steps in the beginning process was to counsel the souls, especially regarding the importance of forgiveness of those who had hurt them, as well as forgiving themselves. When they returned to me during meditation from the Resting Area and said they were ready, with the help of the Heavenly Helpers, we brought them before God (their Higher God Self) for admittance to the Light.

Unfortunately, in my father's case, he was not admitted on several occasions. I felt frustrated as I took it personally if the soul was not admitted. Eventually, the "aha" moment came as to what I was doing wrong. I took the word of the soul that they were "ready" to enter the Light, when in fact, they were anxious to do so, but had not done the work they needed to do. From my earthly human perspective, I trusted and believed but I had no way of knowing for sure. That is why we have Spiritual Guidance, so I asked my Heavenly Helpers if they would let me know when the soul was actually ready and had done what was needed. This made the process so much easier and when I brought a soul before God for admittance to the Light, the door was opened.

I'm sorry that my father's soul had to experience rejection on so many occasions, but I appreciate and thank him for the knowledge it afforded me in how to counsel souls properly. Now souls are automatically guided to the Light when the counseling sessions are over and do not have to go before their Higher (God) Self for approval.

My Friend Susan

The second soul that was brought to me for counseling from the Resting Area was Susan, a friend of mine. Susan was killed in a car accident during our high school years. I remember being extremely upset over her passing even though we were only casual (not best) friends. I remember all the details of her death -- what I was doing, where I was at the time, and how I heard the news of her death. Evidently I had a soul contract with her that I knew absolutely nothing about until later in life when I started working on my spiritual mission. I was surprised to learn that Susan was still in the Resting Area as she had died thirty-five years prior to my learning to do this work. While time is important on Earth, on the Other Side there are no clocks or calendars so it is not as important. What is important is to increase the soul's vibration level by dissolving negativity through Love, Forgiveness, Compassion, etc.

ACTOR SPENCER TRACY

The third soul I was guided to counsel was Spencer Tracy. When he arrived in meditation, he identified himself as Spencer. At the time I had a nephew-in-law by the name of Spencer, but he was a young child and still in physical form. So when I questioned Spencer who, he said "Tracy." I did not even know that he had died, so after our counseling session, I searched the Internet for verification. Yes, he had died. According to Spencer Tracy, he ended up in the Resting Area upon his physical death as he had been unkind to many people during his career as an actor and needed to make amends before being admitted into the Light.

When I inquired why he felt he was now ready to enter Heaven, he said he "knew" that Katherine Hepburn was about to journey to the Other Side and he wanted to be a part of her greeting committee when she arrived. I imagine he had advanced information to know that she would go straight to Heaven and not the Resting Area. I counseled his soul and he was received in the Light before Katherine passed. I'm sure they had a wonderful reunion.

HELP FOR OTHERS

In the beginning, my Spirit Guides would bring to me the soul energy of an entity that needed counseling in order to be released from the Resting Area. However, on some occasions, during a reading session, a client would ask if a deceased loved one was in Heaven or OK? I would mentally ask my Guides and if this soul was either earthbound, an attachment, or in the Resting Area, I would be able to help them. There are no coincidences, as many times when someone contacts me for a reading, they get more than just the reading – they get help for loved ones who have passed on and it is the client's own Spirit Guides who brought them to me.

Chapter 19

PROCESS FOR GETTING SOULS FROM THE RESTING AREA INTO THE LIGHT

If you are interested in working with deceased loved ones and getting them out of the Resting Area, ask your Spirit Guides to research the Akashic Records and let you know if any of your deceased loved ones are residing in the Resting Area. If so, ask if any of them are ready to transition into the Light. If so, ask for assistance from your Spirit Guides or ask that they bring the appropriate assistance to you from the Light.

With the help of the Beings of Light, you need to connect with the soul energy of the individual you will be counseling regarding their transition to the Light.

COUNSELING CONSISTS OF THE FOLLOWING GOALS

1. Explain that you are connecting with them for the purpose of helping their soul enter the Light (Heaven) and to reconnect with their loved ones and soul group members.

2. Tell them the only contraband not allowed in the higher realms is negative energy and that they need to release and let go of any hatred, revenge, bitterness, anger – any negative energy they are holding onto as it serves no purpose to them.

3. The best way to release their negative energy is through the act of forgiveness. Once they are able to forgive not only others, but themselves as well, passage into the higher realms is automatic.

4. Allow your Spirit Guides to let you know when the entity is ready to pass into the Light.

5. If you so desire, express your love for these entities as they transition to the Light.

It is not uncommon for these souls to return to you after their arrival in the Light to thank you for helping them.

PART IV

RETRIEVAL
&
INTEGRATION
OF YOUR SOUL
FRAGMENTS

Chapter 20

WHAT ARE SOUL FRAGMENTS?

The purpose for being on Earth is to learn life lessons, balance karma and grow to higher spiritual levels. This is not easy, as challenges are placed before us to assist us in our learning and growing process. It is during these challenging times that small parts of our soul decide to exit the physical body.

Soul fragments are parts of our soul energy which exit our body during traumatic events or stressful situations. Sometimes those fragments return and reconnect with our physical body and sometimes they do not. When they do return to us, they need to be integrated into the physical body.

WHY MUST WE RETRIEVE SOUL FRAGMENTS?

When our soul energy resides outside of our physical body we feel off-balanced, not whole. We need to bring this part of our energy into wherever it belongs in the body. If these fragments do not return to us or to the Light, they are considered earthbound and they could become an attachment to someone else's energy field. There is no benefit for us if one of our fragments attaches to another human's energy field. It is our soul energy and is not able to grow by being disconnected from our energy.

It is not only very important, but absolutely necessary (as part of the Ascension Process) for humans to retrieve as many of their soul fragments as possible. Even if we have fragments from past lives in other parts of the world that are still earthbound, it is our responsibility to collect them and arrange to have them escorted to the Light. If they are not a part of our soul energy from this lifetime, they need to be escorted to the Light. If they are a part of our soul from this lifetime and do not wish to return to our physical body, they need to be escorted to the Light to join the Parent Soul.

We are assigned a certain amount of soul energy for each incarnation. The amount is determined by our Soul Purpose. The greater the purpose, the more soul energy we will need. This energy will join the physical body every seven years up to the age of twenty-one. At age twenty-one whatever soul energy is required in order to complete our soul mission will occupy our physical body. As we learn and grow spiritually, our soul energy increases in vibration. When fragments depart during traumatic or abusive situations, they are in a very low, negative vibration and most likely will stay earthbound. Souls and soul fragments need an escort in order to return to the Light. If we check with our Spirit Guides during the Retrieval Meditation and ask any missing fragments to return to us and they do not want to, the best course of action is that they be escorted to the Light. The fragment may be restored to a higher vibration and allowed to return to our physical body, or stay in the higher realms with the Parent Soul if we are at a high enough vibration where we do not need it to return in order to complete our mission.

MY PERSONAL EXPERIENCE

I would like to share a personal experience I recently had (November 2012) regarding the return and integration of a soul fragment from my throat chakra.

Upon my return from a trip to Chicago, I went straight to my church from the airport to participate in a fundraising event. A few days later I started to experience flu-like symptoms. I thought this was a result of my hectic schedule and a sign that I needed to slow down. I was sleeping anywhere from twelve to twenty hours a day. No matter how hard I tried I couldn't stay awake. The moment my head hit the pillow I was gone – out like a light. Normally I usually sleep six to seven hours each night. If I am really overtired, I could sleep up to ten hours, but that would be very unusual. For two weeks I was sleeping almost around the clock. I began to worry as I had to cancel three events I had scheduled during those two weeks.

Into the second week of feeling ill, I became aware that the flu-like symptoms were coming one at a time. Originally I woke up in the middle of the night coughing, gagging and choking. It felt as though I had swallowed something, yet nothing was in my throat. Then I experienced a sore throat. I felt this was a result of my coughing and choking so hard. Next the nasal congestion surfaced, which was so thick that even using my neti pot didn't loosen it up. During the second week I experienced a few days of feeling cold and having chills, such as you would experience with a fever. However, I did not have a fever. Finally, I experienced laryngitis-type symptoms, followed by coughing and gagging again to the point of almost throwing up. I happened to be talking with a couple of friends with medical backgrounds, and when I explained my symptoms and how lucky I was that they came one at a time, they said, "The flu is not that kind – it hits you with everything it has all at once."

I decided to meditate and check with my Spiritual Guidance as to what was going on as I was sure I had the flu. If not the flu, then I felt as though it could have been an attached entity or a psychic attack causing these symptoms.

What happened was a part of my Soul from the throat chakra had decided to return to my physical body. I did not know that a fragment was missing, however, I should have suspected as my throat has always been a very sensitive area for me. While I did not consciously meditate in order to reconnect at that particular time, there have been many times in the past when I had invited any of my soul fragments to return. There is a process to groom these fragmented parts before integrating them back into the physical body. Because I was not aware what was happening as the fragment returned, it entered my body at a much lower vibration than my body was currently vibrating at. Therefore, my body was fighting it off as an invasion/infection which resulted in the flu-like symptoms.

The reason I was sleeping so many hours each day was because my soul was returning to the Other Side for grooming and integration work. I was completely bedridden for two weeks while the integration work was going on. Afterwards I still experienced the choking, gagging-type cough from time to time, but not constantly.

In December 2012 I was scheduled to present my Ascension Workshop on the World Peace Cruise to the Caribbean. In May of that year, I was guided to be on this particular cruise, which I thought was for obvious reasons – to participate in World Peace Prayers. This was great and I loved every minute of the cruise, however, when the Universe guides you to something/someone, there are always bonuses involved.

First, I was connected with a very nice lady. We agreed to exchange services while on the cruise. Her specialty was sound healing. I wasn't sure how I was going to benefit from sound healing, but asked her to concentrate on my throat chakra as that was the only area where I was experiencing any difficulty. My new friend along with the Heavenly Helpers finished the integration of my soul energy in my throat chakra and I no longer experienced the cough.

Apparently, in this lifetime, I had given away my power from my throat chakra by keeping silent in the face of conflict instead of sticking up for myself or arguing a point. It was revealed during the healing session that I had done this same thing in at least three other lifetimes. I guess it was time for me to learn a very valuable lesson. I finally got it!

Second, during the Soul Retrieval Meditation part of my class, one of the participants experienced an emotional reaction to bringing one of her soul fragments back. This was a result of a very recent traumatic experience of the participant where the soul fragment exited. The soul fragment heard the call of the human participant and returned. However, the fragment did not have enough time to bring its energy up to a higher vibration during the integration phase. The fragment's love for the human participant and desire to return created a difficult process for both the human and the soul fragment. Her experience was an eye-opener for me to make sure that the soul fragments be encouraged to return to the Other Side for grooming if their energy is at a much lower vibration than that of the Soul in the physical body.

I asked my Higher Self if the soul fragments return to the Other Side and bring their vibration up, would they be allowed to return to the physical soul on Earth? The response was that it would be up to the Committee overseeing the progress of the human on Earth. If they needed the soul fragment in order to complete their mission, then it would return to the human in physical form once its vibration was within equal range to that of its human partner. If the human was doing well and it was "seen" (from the Other Side they have the ability to see the outcome of events before they happen) that the human would easily complete their mission with or without that soul fragment, then the fragment would remain on the Other Side with the Parent Soul.

Chapter 21

MEDITATION TO CALL BACK SOUL FRAGMENTS

This chapter includes a meditation Sananda provided me with to consciously call back soul fragments. However, in order to prepare for the Soul Fragment Retrieval exercise, it is important to participate in a relaxation meditation, which will allow you to have a stronger connection with your Spiritual Team of advisors as well as your sub-conscious mind.

Relaxation Meditation

I am going to count upward from the number one to the number ten, and with every ascending number slowly blink your eyes. Begin by focusing your eyes upward – to where the wall and ceiling meet or towards the sky. Slowly blink your eyes (in slow motion) with every number I count.

(SLOWLY) ….. One ….. Two ….. Three ….. Four   Five ….. (rising higher and higher) ….. Six ….. Seven ….. Eight ….. Nine ….. and ….. Ten!

Now, close your eyes and keep them closed. The purpose of this exercise was to relax your eyelids. Notice how relaxed and comfortable your eyes now feel. Allow that feeling to expand, to multiply, to magnify, to become greater on all levels. Allow your eyelids to become totally and completely relaxed. Take your time. There is no hurry. Just allow you eyelids to relax totally and completely. And as you relax your eyelids, you can allow that feeling of relaxation to flow outward, in all directions, as in imaginary waves or ripples of energy.

Allow a feeling of relaxation to go outward throughout the entire head and face area. Just think about relaxing all the areas of your head and face. Enjoy the relaxation going outward to the entire head area, relaxing the head. Feel the relaxation slowly trickling down to the neck and then to the shoulders, down the arms and into the hands.

Welcome this wonderful feeling of relaxation going down the entire body, to the legs and feet, all the way down to the toes. Your body may feel heavy, or it may feel light. It may be perfectly still or you may notice a slight movement.

As you totally and completely relax, your entire body feels loose and limp – like a ragdoll. You are relaxed to the point where you have released and let go of all the tension from your entire body which will make it easier for you to connect with your Spiritual Team – your Soul & Higher Self, your Spirit Guides, Angels and/or Jesus/Sananda and Archangel Michael for the purpose of assisting you in calling back any soul fragments, which may have left during turbulent times and are now ready to return.

And in a moment, I am going to count upward again from the number one to the number ten in order for you to make a stronger connection with your Spiritual Team and Spiritual Self and to reach a higher level of relaxation and vibration.

This time I will count RAPIDLY!   One ..... Two ..... Three ..... Four ..... Five ..... Six ..... Seven ..... Eight ..... Nine ..... and ..... Ten.

You are now at your own level of relaxation!

Keep your eyes closed as we will now proceed with the Soul Retrieval of any fragments that have released either during this lifetime or any past lifetimes.

Soul Fragment Retrieval Meditation

1. *Ask your Spiritual Team of helpers to join the sub-conscious mind to dig deep into its files and*

- *Reveal three parts of the soul which may have exited – one at a time.*

- *Ask the first part -- why it exited? What happened in your life to cause it to leave?*

- *Is it willing to come back and join the physical soul?*

- *If so, what can you do to make it a more comfortable experience?*

- *If not, is there anything you can do to change things so that it would want to come back?*

- *If not, does it need more time before it will reconsider?*

- *If so, how much time?*

2. *Cradle this part of your soul in your arms and tell it that everything is okay. You have grown and that you would like it to come back and experience the higher level of energy that you have achieved and it too can bask in the glory of Light and Love, which you now have decided is the path you want to follow. As you are cradling this part of your soul make sure to envelop it (as you would wrap a baby in a blanket) with as much LOVE energy as it is able to accept. Allow your Spiritual Team to control the amount of Love downloaded to this part of your soul.*

   Give yourself plenty of time to dialogue with this part of your soul. (Note: You will be guided as to how much time is appropriate for each soul fragment by your Spiritual Team.)

3. Ask your Spiritual Team of helpers to join the sub-conscious mind, once again, to dig deep into its files and

- *Reveal a second part of the soul which may have exited.*

- *Ask the second part -- why it exited? What happened in your life to cause it to leave?*

- *Is it willing to come back and join the physical soul?*

- *If so, what can you do to make it a more comfortable experience?*

- *If not, is there anything you can do to change things so that it would want to come back?*

- *If not, does it need more time before it will reconsider?*

- *If so, how much time?*

4. Cradle this part of your soul in your arms and tell it that everything is okay. You have grown and that you would like it to come back and experience the higher level of energy that you have achieved and it too can bask in the glory of Light and Love, which you now have decided is the path you want to follow. As you are cradling this part of your soul make sure to envelop it (as you would wrap a baby in a blanket) with as much LOVE energy as it is able to accept. Allow your Spiritual Team to control the amount of Love downloaded to this part of your soul.

5. Ask your Spiritual Team of helpers to join the sub-conscious mind to dig deep into its files and

- *Reveal a third part of the soul which may have exited.*

- *Ask the third part -- why it exited? What happened in your life to cause it to leave?*

- *Is it willing to come back and join the physical soul?*

- *If so, what can you do to make it a more comfortable experience?*

- *If not, is there anything you can do to change things so that it would want to come back?*

- *If not, does it need more time before it will reconsider?*

- *If so, how much time?*

6. *Cradle this part of your soul in your arms and tell it that
   everything is okay. You have grown and that you would
   like it to come back and experience the higher level of
   energy that you have achieved and it too can bask in the
   glory of Light and Love, which you now have decided
   is the path you want to follow. As you are cradling this
   part of your soul make sure to envelop it (as you would
   wrap a baby in a blanket) with as much LOVE energy
   as it is able to accept. Allow your Spiritual Team to
   control the amount of Love downloaded to this part of
   your soul.*

7. *For those parts that have exited and are now willing to
   return -- WELCOME them back. Ask your Spiritual
   Team of helpers to assist in the integration process and
   to ensure that the fragmented part(s) are at a compatible
   vibration with your physical soul energy.*

8. *For those parts that have exited and are not ready to return, at this time, ask them to return to the Parent Soul
   in the higher realm from which they came. There are
   angelic escorts to take them HOME if they are willing to
   go at this time.*

9. *And when you are ready you may open your eyes, feeling
   refreshed, fully alert and in the here and NOW!*

When Jesus provided me with the above exercise to retrieve soul fragments, He stated that most humans have at least
three parts missing so focusing on three parts in one exercise

would be appropriate. Once you perform this exercise and get in the habit of daily calling back any energy which might have exited, you should be okay. However, always make sure to check with your own Spiritual Team of helpers to confirm that you are whole – spiritually speaking.

PART V

WHITNEY HOUSTON'S JOURNEY TO THE OTHER SIDE

Chapter 22

A SPECIAL REQUEST FROM SANANDA

I was saddened to hear of Whitney Houston's passing
on February 11, 2012, but didn't think too much more about
it until I watched the special on Oprah's network where she
interviewed Bobbi Kristina (Whitney's daughter) and Gary
and Patricia (Whitney's brother and sister-in-law). During the
interview, both Patricia and Oprah mentioned that at least
Whitney was now at peace. Each time I heard that comment,
my body was riddled with goose bumps. This was a sign to me
that Spirit was trying to get my attention. When I mentally
reached up and asked if my guidance had something to say to
me, the response was "she is NOT at peace – she is earthbound
and very scattered."

Sananda asked that I work with him in counseling Whit-
ney's soul to release her energy from Earth. I tried calling out to
Whitney's soul consciousness to help her journey to the Other
Side, but did not have success. Then I tried to connect with
Whitney's Higher Self (the God part of her on the Other Side),

but did not achieve success with that process either. This did not surprise me as Whitney did not know me and our Higher Self is our gatekeeper (a screen of protection for the soul).

Within a few weeks Sananda came to me in meditation again and asked that I enlist Oprah's assistance in this process because of her connection with Whitney. Needless to say, either Oprah did not get my email message or she ignored it. Oprah does not know me and I imagine her staff members are her physical gatekeepers and screen her mail and only pass on what they believe to be legitimate. Here I was asking Oprah to mentally call out to Whitney's soul and direct her to go to the Light, as she was earthbound when Oprah already thought that Whitney's problems were over and she was at peace.

So I continued to call out to Whitney's soul and Higher Self many times without success. While I am a sensitive person, I did not take the lack of response by these two ladies personally. I knew I had to persist in my efforts to get Whitney to the Light.

On March 30, 2012, Sananda came to me in meditation once again and expressed the urgency of connecting with Whitney's soul to guide her to the Other Side as she had now attached to her daughter, Bobbi's energy. I explained that I had not been successful in my attempts to connect with Whitney's soul energy or with Oprah via email. I asked if He would be able to help me connect with Whitney's Higher Self and then I could take it from there. With the help of Sananda, I did connect with Whitney's Higher Self and through the Higher Self to her earthbound soul energy. As a result of Whitney's desire to stay close to her daughter, Bobbi Kristina, Whitney's soul energy attached to Bobbi Kristina's energy field. While this may sound harmless and natural, it is very harmful. It would have stripped Bobbi of her right to live life and make her own Free Will decisions. Whitney would have continued life in the physical through Bobbi and this would have created Karma to be balanced in a future lifetime. Even though this was not intentional (it was accidental), as Whitney's only intention was to be with her daughter and to protect her, it is still against spiritual laws to manipulate someone else's energy.

When someone is still in physical form and someone in non-physical form tries to manipulate us, we have the right and can use our Free Will in not allowing this to happen. If Whitney's energy was not released from Bobbi's energy field, Whitney would have continued "her" life as she wanted to live it, and most likely Bobbi would have become addicted to drugs as Whitney had been. This may be why Sananda was insistent upon releasing Whitney's soul from Earth.

Jesus/Sananda was Whitney's escort to the Other Side, and she said that she felt very calm and peaceful in His presence. Due to the manner in which Whitney passed, and the low vibration of her soul energy, she was escorted to the Resting Area by Jesus/Sananda.

Chapter 23

COUNSELING FOR WHITNEY'S SOUL ENERGY

JUNE 6, 2012

During meditation this morning, while giving thanks to my Angels and Spirit Guides, Jesus arrived with Whitney Houston's soul energy for the purpose of counseling her so that she could be released from the Resting Area.

The first and most important phase was for her to admit that her death was intentional (a suicide). While our human records indicate an accidental drowning, the Akashic Records (her Life Book of Records) indicated it was a suicide. For her to admit that she intentionally ended her life was the first step in her healing process. She was able to do this during the first counseling session.

Next I informed her that the second and also very important step was to not only forgive herself, but all others who had hurt her.

Coincidentally, the previous night I watched the movie *Bodyguard* again, even though I had seen it many times before. So I reminded her that life on Earth is like a movie. We each have our parts/roles to play and when the movie is over, and we are done acting our parts, we are all friends again. We need to release and let go of any of the anger, hatred, resentment (anything negative) we accumulated during our journey on Earth, as when we participate in our Life Review and meet with our human enemies upon their return to the Other Side, we will definitely see things in a different (more positive) "light" at that point.

Whitney's homework from this session was to work on forgiveness of self and others. Jesus will bring her to me once He feels that she is ready to accept this assignment. I believe we will have a total of three sessions before she will be ready to enter the dimension of Light (what we call Heaven). I knew that Whitney was very comfortable being in the care of Jesus and that she would have a speedy Soul recovery. While they don't have calendars or clocks on the Other Side, it sometimes takes souls literally years of Earth time to transition from the Resting Area to the higher realms.

Whitney had agreed to provide me with information to include in my book – what it was like to be earthbound, an attachment to her daughter's energy field, what it is like to be in the Resting Area, and then her transition to the Light. I am looking forward to receiving this information.

Information Received in Bali
April 14, 2013

During meditation, I very easily connected with my Master Guide, Jonathan. He helped me in connecting with Whitney Houston's Higher Self and then with her soul energy residing in the Resting Area to further counsel her on the art of forgiveness. She was not able to forgive her ex-husband Bobby for how he treated her. She said that he had done things to her that were unforgiveable and that no one even knew about. At that point, I decided she should concentrate on forgiving herself. I thought if she was able to forgive herself first, then it might be easier for her to forgive Bobby.

During the counseling session, I reminded her about life on Earth being a stage and we were each just playing a role/part in order to grow to higher spiritual levels and to help others grow spiritually as well. I explained that we are here to learn lessons and to grow spiritually. Three very important tools to help us get beyond the pain and suffering we experience with individuals and situations are: Love, Compassion and Forgiveness.

It didn't take much counseling effort before she was able to forgive herself. Then we focused on Bobby. Again, I made reference to the movie *Bodyguard* and the fact that at times she wasn't very nice to Kevin Costner. I was indicating that it was a movie and she was playing out the script that was written out for her character. When the movie was over she and Kevin remained very good friends. This is how life is, but in a personal relationship it often hurts when someone is unkind to us, but they are doing what is necessary to help us learn a valuable life lesson. I told her that when she returned to the higher levels of Light and participated in her Life Review she would see that Bobby was playing a role in "real" life for both her and his benefit to grow to higher spiritual levels. She seemed to understand this concept as I felt a wave of peace come over me as we were communicating.

All of a sudden she started to repeat over and over, *"Oh My God!" "Oh My God!" "Oh My God"!* When I asked her, *"What is going on?"* she said, *"Jesus is here to take me to the Light."* Jesus was standing by to escort her to the Light (as He had promised) the instant He felt she was able to bring the energy of forgiveness into her soul. In parting Jesus made the comment, *"We are going to have fun."* I was not quite sure what He meant by that comment, however, since they don't have "stress" in Heaven, what else can there be but FUN!

I am sure when Whitney Houston experienced her Life Review, she was able to see things much differently than she did upon her physical death. Again, she promised to return and give me a quote for this book/chapter regarding her journey from death to being received in the Heavenly Realm.

The energy in Bali was so powerful, the connection with Whitney as well as Jonathan and Sananda was as if they were in the same room with me – no distance at all.

Chapter 24

MESSAGES FROM WHITNEY

THURSDAY, APRIL 18, 2013

"Hi Barbara, this is Whitney again. I want to thank you so much for working with me to get me where I needed to be. Now for the quote for your book regarding my experience:

After Physical Death

"First of all, I didn't know that anyone would be able to know that I had actually committed suicide. I thought it would be undiscovered. In this realm, they only deal with TRUTH and it is truth that is recorded in my Life Book of Records. They do not cover anything up or make excuses depending on who you are. Being famous carries no weight up here.

"I was very surprised to have consciousness after physical death. I was one who thought 'when life is over, it's over.' But that is not true. The first thing I wanted to do was see my daughter, Bobbi Kristina. Once I found her, I stayed with her even when they came to take my body away. I did not want to stay with my

body. *I only wanted to stay with Bobbi. Because my energy was at such a low state, it caused Bobbi to have a hard time being around me. So I tried to get even closer to her – to hug her and tell her that I still loved her and when I did this she totally collapsed. That is when I discovered that she and I were one. Unfortunately, she immediately started to have the same cravings I had. It did not matter to me. Just to be able to have the sensation of peace again through drugs is all I wanted, not realizing the effect it would have on my darling daughter. I would still be attached to her energy if you and Jesus had not rescued me. Thank You! Thank You! Thank You!"*

Arriving in the Resting Area

"I was thrilled when I saw that Jesus was there to take me Home. Unfortunately, I did not know that I had to go through counseling and do homework first. I 'knew' I probably would not go to Heaven and possibly might end up in 'hell.' But I was escorted to the Resting Area by Jesus. It is not a bad or evil place. I found it to be quite refreshing. Jesus helped me so much by bringing me to you and you helped by explaining that forgiveness was the key to getting into Heaven. I was at a point that I didn't think I was ever going to make it, but Jesus persisted. He visited me many times to check and see if I was ready. While we laughed and spoke about many different things, He never criticized or judged me in any way. I knew He was lending me a helping hand by increasing my energy just by being in my vibration. I love him so much. He loves everyone no matter what they do. It is such an honor to have Him take personal interest in my welfare.

"*After our last counseling session in Bali and Jesus came to take me to the Light/Heaven, I cannot explain in words how that felt as it was wonderful. There is no feeling that I have experienced on Earth even when I was high on drugs, when I experienced such a wonderful all-glowing feeling of LOVE. I really can't explain it to you. You have to experience it yourself and then you will know. But there is definitely no feeling on Earth to equate with it.*"

IN THE LIGHT OF HEAVEN

"*I am now in the Light of Heaven and have connected with several of the individuals I knew from Earth in this lifetime as well as other lifetimes. It is amazing how you automatically know and recognize these souls. It is much harder to recognize humans in physical bodies while on Earth. Again, it is hard to explain in words, but there is no stress, worry or fear in this place we call Heaven. There is only Love, Joy, Understanding and Compassion – nothing but positive feelings.*"

A MESSAGE TO OPRAH FROM WHITNEY

"*Please tell Oprah that I love her. I appreciate how she tried to help me and that I have asked Jesus to bring blessings to her. Everyone thinks that because she is Oprah that she has no stress, no worries at all, but she is very concerned about humanity and worries that she is not doing enough to help. As we view her from this realm, we see that she is doing as much as one hundred other individuals together would do, but she is doing it from her heart and soul. This lady has grown spiritually by leaps and bounds in this lifetime. She is truly an Ascended Master and an Earth An-*"

gel. She will not have to return to Earth for additional lifetimes because she has completed so much in this lifetime. However, we feel that she will come back one more time and put the frosting on her mission of helping others."

Upon returning home from my Bali trip, I re-read the information received from Whitney Houston and felt more could be added. Whitney had just arrived in the Heavenly Realm and didn't have enough time to provide any more details. So I called out to her and asked if she would be willing to provide additional information when she was ready. I did not receive a response, and let the idea pass as a "No."

Different Dimensions Described by Whitney
May 24, 2013

However, on May 24th, 2013, I received the washboard-type chills indicating that someone from the Light was trying to get my attention. When I mentally reached up and recognized their call to me, it was Sananda who had brought Whitney's soul energy to me so that she could provide additional information regarding her journey to the Other Side. Following are her comments:

"I now understand why we have to eliminate the negativity we accumulate on Earth, as there is no negativity to deal with on this side. Why we ever decide to come to Earth is a mystery to me. Yes, we grow and are helping others, but the difference between here and there (Earth) is many worlds of difference.

"Anyway, Jesus has shown me around the different dimensions that I am allowed to visit. I am now in the 4th dimension, and I am able to visit the 5th and 6th dimensions for a short period of time with an escort of a higher vibration. There are individuals in those two dimensions that I knew on Earth, but my main residence is the 4th dimension.

"During our visit to the 5th and 6th dimensions, Jesus said that He was showing me where I could end up after my next incarnation on Earth. It will be easier the next time as I have been told that I scheduled too many lessons in my Life Plan for this past lifetime. I will not make that mistake again. While I will have to do my lessons over again in another lifetime, I have already been planning what I will do. Because I was able to forgive Bobby (my ex-husband), I will not have to be with him, but I will have to go through those lessons with another individual. I am not sure when I will return to Earth, but I do know that I will make it to the Ascended Master vibration. I feel really excited about the next time as I was shown in my Life Review what I did to hold myself back – stuck in negativity so that I was not able to move forward. I KNOW I will succeed the next time.

"It has been so wonderful having Jesus taking such a special interest in my progress. He is truly a very loving soul and wants ALL of humanity to succeed during their journeys to Earth. So I WILL definitely return and plan to achieve success as Jesus will work with me as He has been working with you in this lifetime. He oversees the progress of many multi-millions of souls. Many of them do not know that He is a part of their life, but He is.

"During my visit to the 5th dimension, Jesus showed me that all I have to do is think about what I want, and it will manifest immediately. It was fun experimenting with creating things and then dissolving them back into energy before I had to leave that realm.

"During our visit to the 6th dimension, we were still able to manifest whatever we wanted, but it didn't seem as important as it did during my visit to the 5th dimension. Overseeing our loved ones and helping them from the 6th dimension was far more important. So helping those on Earth to manifest their heart's desire was more important. Helping humans with the healing process is also a benefit from the 6th dimension vibration. We can send energy to those who need it if someone has put in a request. We cannot do anything without the individual soul requesting help in some way even if someone else is requesting on their behalf.

"I thank Jesus for taking the time to show me what is to come if I would only listen to my heart and the Spiritual Guidance that is assigned to help me instead of trying to struggle and to do everything myself. That is what got me into the state of mind I was in on Earth and ultimately caused me to end my life. I couldn't take it anymore.

"I will continue to grow spiritually while on this side. Jesus said that I have already grown during the short time I have been here, but I have more growth to achieve before re-entering Earth's journey and that will make the next lifetime much easier to get through.

"I cannot tell you how I feel, how grateful I am to you for helping me to get where I am now. I have never been so happy or felt so fulfilled as a soul wanting to succeed with my life mission. I have not made a blueprint for my next life yet, but Jesus is on my committee and promises to help me create a 'livable' plan.

"I would like to say to all of my fans that I LOVE YOU! I APPRECIATE YOU! And I have asked God to Bless you in order to keep you on your path and enjoying life on Earth. God Bless You ALL!"

At the end of our conversation Whitney asked if she could return to me again to practice her skills of communicating with humans. This is not a talent that all human souls possess until they reach a certain level of vibration (4th dimension). Souls at a lower vibration are able to communicate with humans still in physical form if they are accompanied by a higher vibrational entity to hold the energy for them. Jesus/Sananda and my Master Guide, Jonathan, had escorted Whitney's energy to me during the counseling sessions and for the quotes for this book so they held the energy for her.

However, her request for practice communication was so that she could build her energy to be able to communicate one-on-one without having an escort for support. I imagine this is part of her growth process on the Other Side. I told her I would be honored and happy to "practice" communicating with her.

Final Comments About Whitney
MAY 26, 2013

I should not have been, but I was pleasantly surprised when she returned to practice communicating within a few days (May 26). I asked if she was able to come alone and she said, "No," that Jonathan had been her escort. It was delightful communicating with her. She said that she had asked Jesus, of all the multi-millions of people on Earth, why He brought her to me for assistance in getting her to Heaven as we didn't even know each other. The response was that we had a contract for that purpose. Even if she had not committed suicide, her Life Plan scheduled that her soul would leave Earth before it was time for me to pass. No matter how her soul exited Earth, I had a contract to assist her to the Light. Even though we did not know each other physically, spiritually we are one.

Whitney indicated that Jesus had brought her to the Akashic Records, which revealed that our souls had been together in two different lifetimes. Neither lifetime was in the United States. She said we were together before the United States existed as a country.

I did not take the time to write down everything she said as I did not think it was material for this book. However, Whitney is definitely at peace now and very much aware of what is going on here on Earth.

I have worked with assisting literally hundreds of thousands of souls (with the help of my Spiritual Guidance) to the Heavenly Realm, but not one who has made the progress as quickly as Whitney has. I believe she had made a strong connection with Jesus prior to her passing and He was standing by to assist her to the higher realms. She is a delight to communicate with and I am thrilled that she made such a quick transition to the peaceful place we call Heaven!

My Master Guide Jonathan has informed me that Whitney has made great strides regarding bringing her vibration to a higher level. She misses everyone and wants to express her sincere apologies to not only family and friends, but everyone who knew her, regarding her ending her life so abruptly. She has made amends for this action and is eager to move forward. She was surprised to have Jesus take such a personal interest in her recovery and growth, that she is determined to be successful in her upcoming new life. She was supposed to make it to the Ascended Master vibration during this lifetime. However, as she now knows, she scheduled too many "hard" lessons. She will not do that in her next incarnation. Also, with her staying in the non-physical world in order to grow to a higher vibration, it will make her next journey to Earth so much easier and successful.

During the lifetime that just ended for Whitney she had grown a little beyond the mid-point of the 4th dimension. Upon birth she was at the beginning level of the 4th dimension. During her stay in the 4th dimension, she will grow to the point she was at when she departed Earth and then be reborn into a new physical body, but without the negativity she had accumulated. Things will be different on Earth at that time and life will be easier for all souls.

Many times when I assist/counsel souls in entering the Light from either being earthbound or from the Resting Area, they return and express their thanks and appreciation for my help. I do this work with the guidance of my Heavenly Helpers. It is part of my Soul Contract and I am fortunate to have excellent helpers, without whom I would not have the power to do anything. I would encourage those of you who feel that this is something you would like to do, to connect with your guidance and let them assist you in helping others as well.

JULY 14, 2013

This morning during meditation, Whitney's energy was brought to me once again for the purpose of practicing her communication skills with the human realm. She was commenting about how wonderful it was on the Other Side and still very thrilled that Jesus/Sananda (she now refers to Him as Sananda at His request) was acting as her guide and helping her to raise the vibration of her energy. In order to do this she said that He would escort her to the 5th and 6th dimensions and then bring her back to the 4th. She did not know this, but that is an exercise Spirit suggested I use many years ago in order to raise my vibration. I have passed this along to others, but here I would like to stress the importance of this very easy inexpensive method of spiritual growth.

Exercise: During meditation ask that your Higher Self meet you in the 7th dimension. You are coming for a visit and would like your Higher Self or any Light Being assigned to work with you to be your escort. Imagine that you are getting on an elevator. Press the number 5, 7, or 9 (your Higher Self/ Light Being will know which dimension you chose and will be there when you arrive). When the elevator stops and the doors open, your Higher Self or some other high level Light Being will be there to greet you. Embrace this Being of Light and absorb as much Light energy as possible. Express gratitude to your Higher Self/Being of Light and step back onto the elevator and press the Earth button.

I am very grateful to Whitney for providing confirmation that this is an exercise used on the Other Side for spiritual growth. We too can use this very simple, free, extremely valuable exercise to assist our own spiritual growth while on Earth. Done on a regular basis you will be amazed how good you feel.

Afterword

Soul Releasement work has been very rewarding for me. Why I put it in my Soul Contract, I don't know – possibly because there is such a need for this process at this particular time in Earth's history.

Spirit informs me that there are literally multi-millions of earthbound entities on the planet. I know there are many others who are performing this service, using their own technique. However, my guidance has asked that I put this procedure in book format in order to assist anyone who is experiencing earthbound (ghost) activity or attachment experiences to be able to help themselves.

This procedure is not difficult. However, there are a few necessary requirements before you begin:

- First, it is important that you have the ability to communicate with your Spiritual Team of helpers – Higher Self, Angels, Ascended Masters, Spirit Guides and/or Jesus/Sananda and Archangel Michael or any other Light Beings who are assigned to work with you. If you are not already communicating with your Team, you need to do so as they are the ones providing you with the information you will need to do Soul Releasement work.

- Second, call in your Spiritual Team before you get started and provide them with the necessary information. They may have guidance for you that you are not aware of, such as when I planned to connect with the energy of a relative who had committed suicide, and it would have been detrimental to me to do so. Eventually I did connect with him and released his Soul to the Light. It is so important to listen to our Heavenly Helpers.

- Third, always protect yourself before beginning a Soul Releasement session. It should be your intention to help souls get to the Other Side without them transferring over to your energy field. In addition to using your own protection technique, it would be wise to ask your Spiritual Team to ensure that, if the earthbound entities do not wish to leave, they do not stay with you.

- Fourth, you need to release and let go of any fear you may have of working with deceased entities. If the entity does not want to leave the Earth Plane, you need to stand firm and confident in your counseling session that there is a better place for them to be. If you show fear, you will not be able to convince them to go. Your fearful energy will convince them that you are not being truthful and that they, too, need to "fear" the unknown – that they made the right decision to stay earthbound.

Most people are very uncomfortable talking about death and the afterlife. However, it would be helpful if we could counsel our own loved ones while they are still with us so that they will not be afraid to go upward upon physical death. I have tried to talk with some of my family members about the importance of not staying on Earth after physical death. Because they know of my ability to connect and communicate with Spirit, they thought I had received some "news" about their passing, and it made them quite nervous. I assured them I didn't have any insider information, I was just trying to cut down on the earthbound rate. I only hope that I "remember" to go upward at the time of my physical departure.

I do have some insider information that you may not know about. When we die and our soul does not proceed to the higher realms, by staying earthbound, we are considered "darkness" – not demonic or evil, just darkness. I learned this when I began doing Soul Releasement work. When I started communicating with Spirit, my intention was to only work with Light Beings. I didn't want to give darkness an opportunity to come to me. My Spiritual Team instructed me that I would be working with darkness by working with the earthbound souls. I didn't understand what they meant so I asked them to explain. They said that until a soul returns to the higher dimensions after physical death and are cleansed by the Light, they are considered darkness or negative because of the traumatic, stressful or abusive life experiences they had while on Earth. During meditation if an entity came to communicate with me I would always ask if they were of the Light? If the response was "Yes," I would be happy to communicate with them. However, with the releasement work, if I receive a "No" response, my next question is: "Are you looking to get to the Light?" If the response is "No," I send them away and tell them they can only come back to me if and when they want passage to the Light.

This is one of the best reasons to make sure we do not stay earthbound after physical death. I do not want to be classified as "darkness." Also, earthbound entities cannot plan another physical life for growth purposes. By attaching to another human and living life through them causes Karma which only hinders the spiritual growth process for both souls.

During the counseling sessions with the souls in the Resting Area looking for passage into the Light/Heaven, the one major thing all souls have to do in order to be released is forgive themselves and anyone who has hurt them. Sounds easy enough, however for most souls it is not. There are still many on Earth who need to practice forgiveness in order to make their journey to the Other Side upon death an easy, natural adventure.

Always remember throughout your days, weeks, months and years, the importance of forgiveness. Remember that forgiveness does not absolve the person who has hurt you; it releases you from carrying the burden. You are the beneficiary of forgiveness. If you have not exercised the act of forgiveness, try it. Practice it while on Earth so that when your day comes, you will have direct, clear passage to the Light. I can guarantee that you will feel so much better. Forgiveness was one of my Life Lessons so I am speaking from experience.

IMPORTANT: FORGIVENESS IS THE KEY TO HEAVEN

Every single soul I have counseled from the Resting Area were not released to the Light until they were able to forgive those who had hurt them as well as forgive themselves for any "wrong-doing" while on Earth. Regarding earthbound and attached souls, if they are not able to release their burdens while on Earth, they are guaranteed a ticket to the Resting Area until they are able to do so.

Since we have to "ask" for what we want, I ask God (the Universe) to shower each of you with blessings along your journey here on Earth.

Barbara M. Hardie

ABOUT THE AUTHOR

Barbara M. Hardie is the Founder and Director of Angel Connections, established in 1995 in Tolland, Massachusetts. Her mission is to help individuals open their awareness of who they are spiritually, to find inner strength and peace, to attract abundance, release negative energy which causes stress/problems, improve health and relationships, and to improve the quality of life in general through spiritual awareness.

She is an Ordained Spiritualist Minister, Certified Spiritual Healer, Medium and Counselor through The National Spiritual Alliance. She lectures on a variety of spiritual topics, channels the Ascended Masters and Archangels, and offers phone or email sessions designed to help individuals reach higher levels of vibration. Her first book *Creating Heaven on Earth: A Guide to Personal Ascension* received two Finalist Awards one from Best Books - USA Book News and the other from International Book Awards.

She is a Certified Master Hypnotherapist and received her certification through IACT – International Association of Counselors and Therapists. Barbara Hardie has combined her business experience, hypnotherapy skills and spiritual awareness in developing the programs offered by Angel Connections.

From October 1997 through January 2007 she organized/ sponsored/promoted from one to five Mind-Body-Spirit Expos each year throughout New England and New York which she used as a venue to present information on *Soul Releasement: Assisting Souls into the Light,* as well as *Creating Heaven on Earth: A Guide to Personal Ascension.*

Barbara has lectured on spiritual topics and specifically the information contained in her books for the past 18 years to groups large and small throughout New England – in Massachusetts, Connecticut, Vermont, New Hampshire, Maine and Rhode Island; as well as in Albany, New York, Allentown, Pennsylvania, West Palm Beach, Florida, Chicago, Illinois and Bend, Oregon. During 2006, 2007, 2009, 2012 and 2013, she presented workshops and provided spiritual readings on the Royal Caribbean and Celebrity Cruise Lines to destinations in the Caribbean, Spain, Italy and France in Europe, as well as Alaska and Hawaii.

Visit www.angelconnections.com to learn more about Barbara. If you would like to schedule a private session or have a specific question, please email Barbara at barbara@angelconnections.com.

Additional Offerings from Barbara M. Hardie

BOOKS

Soul Releasement: Assisting Souls into the Light (September 2013)

Creating Heaven on Earth: A Guide to Personal Ascension (July 2011)

ANGEL READINGS

Allow the Angels and Spirit Guides to help you in knowing and understanding the situations that you are experiencing in your life. Feel free to ask questions about any or all areas of your life (60- or 30-minute phone or email sessions).

SOUL PURPOSE READINGS

Who are you? What are you supposed to be doing? Why are you here? Are you on your spiritual path? At this time many are restless, curious about what they are supposed to be doing. Let your Spiritual Guidance put you at ease, knowing what your purpose/life mission is for this lifetime (60- or 30-minute phone or email sessions).

The Angel Readings and Soul Purpose Readings can be combined into one session.

REMOTE SOUL RELEASEMENT SESSIONS

Soul Attachments

If you think or feel that you have an entity or entities attached to your energy/auric fields, Barbara Hardie can check to see if this is the case. If so, she can release them and have them escorted to the Light and then cleanse and groom your energy from any residue of negative energy the entity/entities may have left behind. (This session can also be done from a distance and is usually done in the early morning hours.)

EARTHBOUND SOULS

If you know of an individual who has passed from physical form to spirit and they have not gone to the Light, Barbara Hardie can assist their Soul to their new home on the Other Side. (This work can be done remotely through meditation and connecting with the deceased individual's soul energy.)

RELEASEMENT FROM THE RESTING AREA

If a loved one has passed and you want to know where they are and if they arrived in the Light, Barbara Hardie can check on their whereabouts. If they are in the Resting Area (an area where the soul goes when they are carrying a lot of negative energy), Barbara counsels your loved one until such time as they are ready to be received into the Light.

Visit www.angelconnections.com
Sign Up to Receive Special Alerts and Offers
Email barbara@angelconnections.com to:
Order additional copies of Soul Releasement
and to order Creating Heaven on Earth
Schedule private sessions or request pricing.

Made in the USA
Middletown, DE
11 November 2018